The ABC of Child Protection

The ABC of Child Protection

Jean Moore

LONDON AND NEW YORK

First published 1992 by Ashgate Publishing

Reissued 2018 by Routledge
2 Park Square, Milton Park, Abingdon, Oxon, OX14 4RN
52 Vanderbilt Avenue, New York, NY 10017

Routledge is an imprint of the Taylor & Francis Group, an informa business

Copyright © J Moore 1992

All rights reserved. No part of this book may be reprinted or reproduced or utilised in any form or by any electronic, mechanical, or other means, now known or hereafter invented, including photocopying and recording, or in any information storage or retrieval system, without permission in writing from the publishers.

Notice:
Product or corporate names may be trademarks or registered trademarks, and are used only for identification and explanation without intent to infringe.

Publisher's Note
The publisher has gone to great lengths to ensure the quality of this reprint but points out that some imperfections in the original copies may be apparent.

Disclaimer
The publisher has made every effort to trace copyright holders and welcomes correspondence from those they have been unable to contact.

A Library of Congress record exists under LC control number: 92033655

ISBN 13: 978-1-138-34326-9 (hbk)
ISBN 13: 978-1-138-34330-6 (pbk)
ISBN 13: 978-0-429-43925-4 (ebk)

Contents

Acknowledgements vi
Preface vii

PROLOGUE

1 The battered child 3

A: FOUR FACES OF CHILD ABUSE

2 The first 'great concern' – physical abuse 13
3 Children in the shadows – marital violence 37
4 Tabloid turbulence – sexual abuse 46
5 Neglect of neglect – child neglect 80

B: THE WORKER

6 The worker *with David Divine* 97
7 A misassessment of black families in child abuse work *Emmanuel Okine* 114

C: STRATEGIES

8 Face-to-face work with the abused child 127
9 Legal strategies *Caroline Ball* 140
10 Child protection skills 154
11 Child protection conferences 162
Epilogue 179

Appendix 180
References 184
Index 199

Acknowledgements

So many people have played a part in the writing of this book. My grateful thanks must go to Beryl Day who in this and so many projects has offered her support and encouragement. Warmest thanks must go to Alison Leake who struggled tirelessly with my syntax and content. Ivy Pestell deserves special thanks for undertaking all the irritating jobs that have to be done before a book reaches the publisher. My gratitude is extended to all the professionals who have attended my courses and have taught me so much, and to Joan Searl who has typed untiringly manuscript after manuscript. Last but most significantly my thanks to Peter my husband who created the space in a very busy life so that the book could be written.

Preface

My original intention was to add a new chapter to *The ABC of Child Abuse Work* to acknowledge the changes emanating from the 1989 Act. Instead, stimulated by professionals attending courses, I began to write an entirely new book, leaving *The ABC of Child Abuse Work* to remain in its own right. I chose the title *The ABC of Child Protection* not only to use the current terminology but to emphasize that any understanding of child abuse must be used to create skills to protect children and understand abuse through the eyes of the child.

I have echoed one or two thoughts in the prologues of both books so they can become companion volumes.

PROLOGUE

PROLOGUE

1 The Battered Child

Child abuse is such a painful subject that it is easy for the child to get lost. Unconsciously, trying to avoid the pain, workers get enmeshed in policy meetings, endless re-drafting of procedures and turgid discussions concerning criteria for registration. Recent inquiry reports have emphasized how professionals have been diverted from their main task of protecting children. Jasmine Beckford and her sister Louise were 'regarded as mere appendages to their parents who were treated as the clients' (A Child in Trust 1985). The case conference in the case of Tyra Henry (Whose Child 1987) 'paid very little attention to Tyra and her needs', and finally in the case of Kimberley Carlile the worker 'lost sight at times of the possibility of child abuse' (A Child in Mind 1987).

Part of the problem is that it is not easy to focus on the child when the child inside the parent is crying so loudly. We therefore miss the tears of the abused child. So let's begin by focusing on the battered child.

This is not a simple task. Children can also be abused by poverty, poor housing, inadequate health facilities and attitudes of racism, sexism and classism. It is not easy therefore to discover to what extent the long-term difficulties displayed by a child are due to an identified act of abuse or to the insidious effects of the child's situation and environment. We also know now that the non-injured siblings of the abused child are at risk 'of long-term problems' (Lynch and Roberts 1982).

CUMULATIVE EFFECTS

The story of Mary Edwards clearly shows that the problem is not just the physical pain of the original abuse, but also that the continuing effects of cruelty can lead to a lifetime of damaging interactions. Mary was blinded in one eye by her mother when she was a toddler and was scarred by cigarette burns on her thighs. She was removed and placed in care:

> The eye was a great stumbling block to my social and emotional development. At the age of ten I became very aware of my eye, as it was opaque. I felt ugly, different, nobody wanted to look at me. How could anyone love someone with a funny eye? That's why I haven't got a family, I thought. I remember constantly wanting to be loved. I longed to go to bed early to escape from reality into my fantasy world. I conjured up this beautiful image of a woman with an eternal smile – all-understanding, all-patient, with nothing to do all day but to sit and cuddle me. When morning arrived I was angry – resented the intrusion of real people.

Mary resented the staff in the children's establishment and could not accept the overtures of her foster parents who, after a series of incidents, asked for her to be removed. At seven she frequently truanted from school. She already had problems with men and on one of her absences from school, she met a man who sexually abused her:

> I didn't know what he was trying to do but I know I didn't like it, as he hurt me. I lay like an obedient child and when he finished my reward was money which I immediately spent on sweets.

Mary's early teens were chequered by self-denigrating behaviour and when told about her early abuse and the imprisonment of her mother she said 'I resolved, I'm the daughter of a jailbird. No wonder nobody wants me. The people who were kind were so because they were paid to look after me.'

THE PAIN OF INTERACTION

It's easy for the lay public to believe that the problem can be solved by a successful prosecution and removal of the child into care. Seen through the child's eyes however, the picture is very different. Suddenly strangers arrive. You are in hospital. Painful tests take place 'in order to make you better.' You know what rules to follow at home to avoid further hurt but here the rules are different and confusing. Just as you are settling down you go to a foster home. More strange faces. You think 'This is all my fault, if I'd tried harder and been really good none of this would have happened.' You get to know and trust one social worker, then she leaves the office to have her own baby. This is a prelude to a whole string of workers who are responsible for 'your case', until you leave care. At last you get rid of all the officials but, having longed to escape, you find the world is a very lonely place. Your parents don't want you, but you hope perhaps they may have a change of heart. Each of your trips home is yet another rejection.

LONG-TERM EMOTIONAL EFFECTS

No one person's experience can ever be fitted into neat compartments but perhaps the long-term emotional effects can be divided into the following five responses, with some children using all responses at different times.

Hyperactive children

There are children who have learnt to cope by being negative, aggressive and action-orientated, always on the go with manic activity. These children often have short attention spans and an exceptionally low tolerance of frustration. They are rough with other children, their own and others' toys. The phrase 'clumsy of danger' seems to fit them as they seem to invite accidents. They remain almost rigidly quiet and then erupt into action, perhaps bursting into uncontrollable bouts of temper that terrify themselves, other children, and especially their caretakers. They are the sort of children who the parents set up to be the focus of all the family's rage and encourage the other siblings to also batter and reject the child. It then becomes easy for them to seek pain and provoke violence perhaps as a release from the chronic tension of their social environment.

Fred Crompsall

Fred could be understood through the use of this model. He always reminded me of a tortoise standing on its hind legs; his head jutted in and out between hunched up shoulders. But here the resemblance ended. The last thing that could ever be said was that Fred was slow – Fred always did everything at breakneck speed; he was never still; he needed to be constantly on the move and destructive. No child or child's toy was safe from Fred. He wreaked havoc wherever he went. After the briefest of pauses when he was momentarily still, his next foray would begin with a painful tug of a child's hair or a poke in the ribs.

Fred was beaten by his mother who had a great need to control. When out shopping with her he resembled a wooden toy soldier, but both he and his mother needed him to burst through the short-lived facade so that he could be attacked again. Mrs Crompsall violently resented the passivity and ineptitude of her husband who was able to evade his parental and marital responsibilities by working for a multinational firm that took him away from home most of the year. When he did return, the husband would periodically evade his wife's verbal attacks by getting drunk and then beating her and Fred. Fred's sister, however, was always spoilt and adored. Children like Fred identify with the aggressor and are most likely to suffer subsequent abuse and to be unsuccessful in foster placements. They will 'try to provoke the foster parents into abusing and rejecting them rather than wait for the inevitable (they believe) abuse and rejection to occur' (Doyle 1990).

Passive children

In contrast, some children use the ploy of being completely passive, obediently accepting whatever happens to them. After all, it is safer not to try than to risk exposing yourself to further attack. These are children who withdraw and avoid situations including physical contact. Even when absorbed in a game there is no spontaneous chatter. They sit passively bolt upright on their parent's knees, and have a stoic, listless, apathetic quality. These are children who learn very early in life that to lie passive is the answer, perhaps the only answer, and the best way to get food and care in a hostile and chaotic environment where parents are preoccupied with their own needs.

Parental extensions
There are some children who are like small shacks built as extensions to the main house. They are extensions of their parents, and are not valued as people in their own right. These children are not expected to have their own personality, their whole world is to search out and try to fulfil their parents' wishes. The child's very existence may depend on his or her ability quickly to become aware of the nuances of the parents' moods. To be slow on the uptake can have painful results. When young, these children can be spotted by the well-known description 'frozen watchfulness'. They can be charming and well behaved but behind the facade there is a chronically low self-esteem. This is the child whose main purpose in life can become the care of his or her parents. One of my colleagues has drawn a cartoon depicting this response. It was of parents being pushed in a pram by the baby.

Ice-centred children
These children have many of the characteristics already described in the previous category. They are difficult to detect as they appear to be almost unscarred by their earlier experiences. They are certainly easily missed in a busy classroom or children's home. They appear to function well on the outside, but are completely cold on the inside and are incapable of forming warm relationships. One coping mechanism they use is to excel at one particular area of endeavour, but they find no satisfaction in the exercise because they are lonely, joyless children who have missed out on the fun of normal childhood. Because of their composure they can become the focal point of their parents' fantasies and be cast in the role of god or devil to be idolised and then beaten as the family system decrees.

Mandy
Mandy was just such a child. She had an almost Victorian china doll face with straw blonde hair. In care she never became angry, hardly ever cried and if she laughed it appeared to be soulless. She always played by herself; a neat orderly sort of play. Her conversation was like that at a cocktail party, full of acceptable situational phrases.

'I must be bad' children
These children turn all the pain and trauma on to themselves and take all the blame.

Sukina

Sukina aged five died following a sustained and ferocious attack by her father. 'The incident began with the father asking Sukina and her sister to spell their names which they would not or could not do ... the father then hit Sukina on the head with a ruler repeatedly.' After this Sukina was hit by a length of rigid plastic tubing and finally by a length of kettle flex. At least 50 blows were rained on Sukina. At one stage 'when she was too weak to stand' she tried to crawl out of the room to the stairs, asking her father not to hit her. The attacks continued until she was barely conscious. At this stage the parents put her into a bath of warm water to revive her. Sukina tried to lift herself but as she slipped into unconsciousness she told her father 'she was sorry'. As the report stated Sukina 'like so many abused children before her was coping with the feeling that what had happened, was her fault' (Sukina 1991).

Jalil

Playing in the sandpit with a primary school aged child I thought I might be able to help Jalil through his strong feelings of guilt by putting responsibility for the abuse he had suffered where it belonged. Together we created a really bad man who did lots of wicked things. We both enjoyed acting this out together. I then introduced the fact that the bad man was also cruel to his children. Jalil became thoughtful. We then created a judge who would punish the bad man for his crimes of burglary. Jalil and I agreed that the burglary was not the fault of the house owners who had lost their belongings, but was the burglar's fault. However, when our 'villain' was going to be punished for beating his children, Jalil could stand it no longer and shouted, 'The children made him beat them' then very quietly he said, 'It was all their fault, it was all my fault'.

Kelly

Kelly, aged four, who had been beaten by Simon her stepfather with a tent pole because she couldn't write straight, expressed similar feelings.

> Simon said no-one loved me, everybody hated me. I tried to ask my mum if she loved me and she said yes. But Simon said no, she doesn't love you, she wants to get rid of you. Simon told me to jump off the balcony and he locked mum in the room and me on the balcony and he stood there and

laughed, thinking it was funny. I thought no-one loved me so what was the point of living and I tried to climb on to the balcony but I wasn't tall enough. Always I thought I'd done something wrong but I didn't know what I'd done.

Battered children often suffer from self-hate. They pull aggression on to themselves and mutilate themselves either literally or symbolically. Mary Edwards tried to commit suicide. Green (1978) studied 59 abused children and found that 40.6 per cent exhibited self-destructive behaviour. The mean age of the abused children was 8.5, five had made suicide attempts and twelve were self-mutilators.

OTHER EFFECTS

As well as emotional effects there may be long-term physical damage. Martin (Martin et al 1974) found that 53 per cent of the children studied had some neurological abnormality at a follow-up assessment. Lynch and Roberts (1982) however only found 10 per cent of the physically abused children with severe neurological impairment and 15 per cent with moderate impairment but in a later study spoke of a significant amount of permanent visual impairment, squints, and 'loss of visual acuity' (Lynch 1988). Growth failure and failure to thrive often accompany child abuse. Lynch (1988) also states that in her study 10 per cent of the children had persistent growth failure but adds 'however in these children growth failure was likely to be associated with developmental and behaviour problems.'

The area of development most likely to be affected adversely is that of language, so it is not surprising that teachers report abused children to be under-achievers and to have learning difficulties (Lynch 1988). Added to all this, Oates (Oates et al 1985) showed that abused children had few friends.

SURVIVORS

One intriguing area is the child who survives, without physical or neurological damage: 23 per cent according to Lynch

(1988). She suggested that one possible protective factor was the possession of an above average intelligence. Being intelligent the children are more able to perceive and meet parental expectations. They were free of long-term neurological deficit and their 'placement changes were few'. However, there have not been sufficient long-term studies to discover whether damage manifests at a later stage.

TO SUM UP

Martin and Beezley (1977) echoed by Lynch and Roberts (1982) summed up the long-term effects as being inability to have fun, psychiatric symptoms, low self-esteem, learning problems, withdrawal and depression, opposition/defiance, hypervigilance, compulsivity, pseudo-mature behaviour and developmental delay. A very sad list indeed.

A

FOUR FACES OF CHILD ABUSE

The ancient Roman god Janus had only two faces. Sadly, child abuse has many faces. Limitation of space only allows us to look at four. So such important areas as emotional abuse and failure to thrive have had to be omitted. As sexual abuse causes so much anxiety this area of work has been given extra focus.

2 The First 'Great Concern' – Physical Abuse

The more knowledge one has the less sure one becomes. This is precisely the position with our understanding of physical abuse of children. Literally millions of words have been written on the subject. Building on some comments by Lask (1987), what tends to happen when a body of knowledge starts to accrue is a journey through four stages.

The first is the pioneering stage when professionals start to campaign to bring a problem to the notice of colleagues. Then comes the period when everyone tries to climb on the bandwagon. This is followed by the omnipotence period when the profession creates its own gurus who jet around the country lecturing to prestigious conferences. Lastly, comes the fourth stage, which at the time of writing, is where we are now in the case of physical abuse of children. This is the time of disillusionment when we become less sure – even admitting our lack of certainty. 'Yet despite all that has been written, our state of knowledge is not good' (Jones et al 1987). To gain understanding amidst the shifting sands it helps to establish at least one sure platform from which to start. Some constructs may help. (See Figure 2.1.)

FIRST CONSTRUCT – MOVING CIRCLES

Without falling into the trap of blaming the victim it should be taken into account that there may be things about the child,

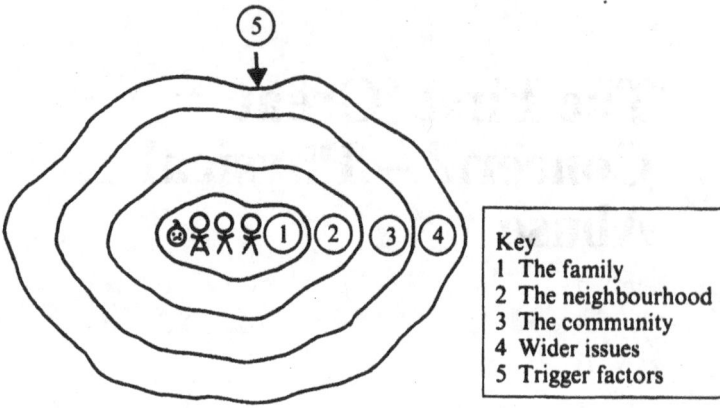

Figure 2.1

the child's behaviour, or at least in the parents' perception of the child's behaviour that results in a negative response from the parents or caretakers. This in turn pulls from the child a negative response. Child, parent and wider caretakers thus become part of a family system (1), which interacts with the neighbourhood circle (2), which in turn responds and is affected by the community (3), and wider issues (4). Without pushing the construct too far, it is like a mobile hanging from the hood of a baby buggy, it moves in the wind and creates unique patterns and shapes.

Physical abuse of children is caused by a variety of interacting and interlocking forces. All may appear well. The tinder wood is dry and there is no sign of fire. Then a trigger factor becomes the match. The fire is lit.

The trigger factor may occur a thousand miles away. An accountant in Chicago looks at the books of a subsidiary firm in a small town in the UK. It isn't making a profit. It must close. Joe has a role in this firm. He is proud of the firm's football team and of his work as shop steward. Suddenly after years of loyal service he is out of work. He never saw himself as a child carer but now his wife has to work. In *his* world the man is the breadwinner but her skills are in demand. Joe feels washed up, devalued and most importantly of all, angry. His marriage, which has always been tenuously balanced, starts to come apart at the seams. Michael, his toddler, who was the reason for the marriage in the first place, is particularly bothersome. Suddenly Joe loses control and attacks the child.

HISTORICAL PERSPECTIVE

Child abuse is as old as time itself. The practice of infanticide was widely accepted among ancient and prehistoric peoples as a legitimate means of dealing with unwanted children. Hilarion's instructions to his wife Alis (1 B.C.) were 'If, as may well happen, you give birth to a child, if it be a boy let it live, if it be a girl expose it' (De Mause 1974). Sexism indeed! The Greek dramatist Euripides recounts that infants were exposed on every hill and roadside 'a prey for birds, food for wild beasts to rend' (Robin 1982). Though Tardieu wrote a paper in Paris in 1860 about his findings on 32 children who were killed by whipping and burning, John Caffey (1946), a radiologist, is usually given credit for initiating the medical world's first 'great concern'.

He noted in 1946 multiple fractures to the long bones of six children suffering from chronic subdural haematoma. It is interesting and says a lot about the attitudes at the time that he was mystified as to the cause. Silverman in 1953 suggested in a later article that it was due to negligence on behalf of the caretakers but softened his observations by suggesting that the injuries may be due to 'accident proneness' (Silverman 1953). It was too painful to consider the parents may be reponsible.

Kempe, with four of his colleagues, coined the phrase 'the battered baby syndrome'. We should be grateful to Kempe (1962) as often it needs a dramatic label to ensure public attention. Something that has been going on for years can then be studied and possible solutions discovered. However he has also left us with the unfortunate legacy of a terrible temptation to see child abuse victims as always young. No one is interested in the six foot victim with a way-out hairstyle. He/she cannot possibly be abused!

WHY?

Adolescents
Referring back to the figure on p 14, let us start, in the

very centre of our first circle (1). The battered child could be an adolescent. Abuse can begin for the first time at this age. Adolescence as a developmental stage can bring a new element into a situation. Garbarino (1980) suggests that this is most common in families when the child was originally indulged by the parents. Parents thus expect excessive dependence and compliance from their offspring. As the child reaches adolescence both parents and children elicit frustration, resistence and anger from each other. The adolescent wants now to be his or her own person. This is when the parents can respond by becoming violent. In half of the cases studied by Garbarino where adolescents were reported for the first time as abused, there was no previous childhood history of abuse.

The saddest group (40 per cent) however, were cases reported for the first time when the child was adolescent but where abuse had been going on throughout the whole of childhood.

The third pattern of adolescent abuse included situations where parents had always used physical chastisement, but as the adolescent was getting bigger, had greater confidence and increased independence, the parents, perhaps feeling they were losing control, escalated their punishments to frightening levels. It is often a last-ditch stand to save a family from real or imaginary disgrace from a 'disobedient' son or daughter.

Sometimes the tables are turned. Parents who have always severely abused, build up considerable resentment in their children. One day the children reach the stage when they can actually resist. This is when they turn on the parent. In cases of matricide and patricide always look first to see if it is the result of long-standing abuse (Mones 1985).

The last pattern to be found in cases where adolescents had been abused is where parents had problems around issues of dependence, autonomy and social control, when the young person was a toddler. The problems of the 'terrible twos' resurrect when the young person reaches adolescence. Now the outcome is more destructive. According to Carlson

> a relationship has been observed between being abused as an adolescent and externalizing or antisocial behaviours, the most common of which is physical aggression or violence .... The consequences are also manifested in internalizing behaviour such as withdrawal, depression, suicidal thoughts ... and self destructive behaviours such as substance abuse (Carlson 1991).

Physical factors

A hyperactive child can become a focal point of the parents' aggression. If there are family and friends around, the parents may be able to cope. If the parent is isolated and already has feelings of low self-esteem she/he experiences an inability to cope, thus confirming all the feelings of low self-image and inadequacy.

Parents may have longed for a responsive bright-eyed child and then it turns out to be placid and unresponsive. It is not necessarily the severely handicapped child that is the focal point of aggression since parents can in these circumstances get a lot of support from services, friends and family. More problematic can be the situation where there is a slight handicap: a child say, with a hearing problem. We tend to discipline by tone of voice. If a child cannot pick up the subtle change of tone, a negative interaction can begin. 'He hears when he wants to' was the angry comment made to me by one mother.

A child's particular pitch of cry can challenge the self-control of adults the world over – from Bangkok to Basingstoke. Nothing, but nothing stops it. A parent can try everything. To some parents, however, the child seems to be rejecting the very essence of their care. They longed for the day they could cuddle the baby. It turns out to be a non-cuddler. To add insult to injury, it spits out its food. The child may be seen as the wrong sex or believed to be different in some way. For instance James' mother overhead a conversation in the hospital which implied, she thought, there was something wrong with her son. She began to insist he *was* different. Certainly his odd haircut and untidy clothes were in sharp contrast to the presentation of his pretty sisters. Shortly after the birth of the third child she admitted she had tried to strangle James.

The child may become a symbol

Some people make excellent partners but cannot take into a relationship a third person – a child. The child then becomes a symbol of the broken relationship. 'All was well till you arrived.' A child can be seen as a bearer of trouble and bad luck; born at a time of crisis. Or a child can be a reminder of a painful past. Donna had been beaten by her father for stealing. She was eventually sent to prison in adulthood for theft. She then settled into a respectable relationship. Then when her child stole 50p from her boyfriend's trousers hanging over a chair, all her painful past flashed through her mind and she attacked the child, breaking his collar bone.

Bonding

It would be going over the top to suggest that if bonding doesn't take place in the first 30 minutes of life the child will be battered. However bonding, though always remembering the comments of Sluckin (1983), is crucial. If parents and child have suffered experiences that interfere with the attachment it can create significant difficulties. Jones (1987) cites the case of Brenda, aged 26 who was effective in her job and meticulous in her home. She successfully reared a placid and obedient little girl but her second child was a premature boy who had to spend three weeks in an incubator in a neonatal unit many miles from the parents' home. She didn't establish an emotional relationship with the child. As so often happens she blamed the victim, saying she found him unresponsive and difficult. She attempted to strangle him one night 'after many weeks of sleeplessness because of his crying.'

The difficulty with all the studies that have been published is that though we can perhaps distinguish 'abusing parents from the total population' (Jones et al 1987) the features are not significantly different from those parents having general problems with their children. However to aid study, a second construct may be helpful.

SECOND CONSTRUCT – THE HOUSE

Think of a house that has many rooms. In each room can be found parents or caretakers who may be more vulnerable to abusing their children.

Hostile pedigree

Go through the front door and into the first room of the house. Here I would put parents who have been brought up in an atmosphere of emotional deprivation where they have been unloved, assaulted themselves, where violence has been the main way of problem solving in *their* homes. They have no model of love and have often been bonded in hate to parents who denigrate them as people or as parents. They cannot break free, their parents keep them tied in a relationship that undermines them and their parenting skills. This often leads to hostility towards all authority figures, to seeing the world as distrustful, and to a good deal of unprocessed anger. Such people may present well as workers and friends, to adults. However when children are born, and especially during the toddler stage, the child appears to hold the key to the cupboard of anger, which when it is unlocked can envelope the child.

Excessive dependence needs
Close the door and go along the corridor, to the room containing the group of parents who have excessive dependence needs – searching for love at any price. They cannot maintain relationships as they drain everyone dry, workers included. They are so desperate to keep a relationship that when the violent partner moves in they will sacrifice the child to keep the partner (as has been found in so many inquiry reports).

Role reversal
Proceed to the next room and here I would put the people who demonstrate the phenomenon of role reversal. All their unsatisfying lives they have longed for the time when they will have a child who will magically transform their whole world. Babies of course don't do that, at least not in the way we expect. Children are demanding creatures. The parent then experiences the child's demands as irritating and unwelcome. The more the child is ignored, the more the child claws for attention. The child who was going to make all things well and good, is seen as a little monster. Once this line of thinking develops, the child is seen as deserving of attack.

Too high expectations
In the next room would be adults who have too high expectations of children's developmental milestones. They expect the child to be clean too quickly, to walk too soon. At a very early age they expect the child to know right from wrong. One mother with a child of three months angrily said 'He knows right from wrong – he's just being difficult to get back at me.'

Rigid and obsessive
It's time we went upstairs. In the front bedroom I would put

parents who are rigid and obsessive. They have coped successfully, sometimes very successfully, with their professional lives. Then baby arrives. They read all the right manuals but this new little person skews their well-ordered existence and untidies their beautifully kept home. The child throws his meal on the floor. It is mopped up. He then wets the shiny parquet floor. It is mopped up. Then the last straw, he sicks all over the expensive wall covering. Perfect routines and domestic standards are thrown into chaos. The child is battered.

Marital conflict and stress
We rush on quickly to the next bedroom. Lorber (Lorber et al 1984) teases out marital conflict and family discord as a predisposing factor to physical violence. Millner and Wimberley (1980) and Whipple and Webster-Stratton (1991) talk about the effects of being under a high degree of stress. Lily's marriage was on the rocks. Her husband spent most of his evenings out. She guessed where. Her anger and frustration were visited upon the baby. She really regretted her actions each time she hit the child but she couldn't control herself. The trouble was her guilt made her cuddle the child afterwards. Inadvertently she was teaching the child an awful lesson. You can only get love after you have been hurt.

The trouble with violence is that it has a momentum all of its own. The rhythm of the attack releases even more violence and the abusers can often be really shocked by the results of their actions. 'I couldn't have done that' is a common response when shown the photograph in court.

Munchausen syndrome by proxy
In the small bedroom are parents who do not abuse their children but get the doctors to do it. Let me explain. For incredibly complex reasons a parent, usually the mother, according to Mehl (Mehl et al 1990), presents the child to the doctor, with an illness, that has been factitiously produced. The term Munchausen syndrome by proxy (Meadow 1977, 1982, 1985) is named after the eighteenth-century Baron Karl Frederich Von Munchausen whose fame derived from his widely exaggerated tales and adventures. Often the child becomes incredibly close to the parent and thus symbiotically participates in the process. So the parent goes to the GP and

complains the child is in pain. The doctor tries to reassure that the child is all right. The parent returns and makes veiled threats about professional neglect. The doctor, to calm the parent, suggests a urine test. The parent doctors this, by putting in a drop of her own blood. On other occasions diarrhoea may be produced by excessive administration of laxatives. Inappropriate and often painful tests begin. One child (Jones et al 1986) had 33 blood tests, eight urine tests, nine stool tests and four radiological tests before the two-year-old was diagnosed as suffering from Munchausen syndrome by proxy.

Sometimes, totally unnecessary operations take place and the child dies on the operating table. In one small study (Meadows 1982) the mortality rate was found to be 10 per cent. The psychological consequences to the child are also serious.

Obviously this condition is hard to discover. The mother is likely to be especially attentive when the child is in hospital. She may form close relationships with the staff, so much so that other parents think she is on the pay roll. Hospital staff are often reluctant and sometimes angry when the possibility of Munchausen syndrome by proxy is mentioned.

Parents often deny when confronted. 'Some parents admit their guilt with relief and accept psychiatric intervention. Others attempt suicide, become psychotic or seek surgery for themselves' (Palmer and Yoshimura 1984). Little is known about the fathers. The literature sees them as weak, inconspicuous and often unaware of the fabrications, as they are not closely involved with their children and rarely visit during hospitalization.

The last two rooms

In the two remaining boxrooms there are two small groups of parents. It is estimated that less than 10 per cent of all children are abused by parents who could be described as mentally disturbed (Kempe and Helfer 1972). There is also a small group of people prescribed tranquillizers who after having taken high doses can have outbursts of rage which are in sharp contrast to their usual lethargy. It is on these occasions that the child can become vulnerable. Let's leave the house and look at family patterns.

FAMILY PATTERNS

Families come in all shapes and sizes. There can be one parent of either sex, two parents or multiple carers. Tolstoy in *Anna Karenin* stated enigmatically that 'all happy families resemble one another, each unhappy family is unhappy in its own way.' Some of the patterns to emerge in battering families are as follows.

Transgenerational abuse
A grandmother was a very poor mother to her daughter who now has a child of her own. All the earlier problems between the grandmother and her daughter are resurrected. The daughter becomes jealous of her own mother who is enjoying proving herself to be a better mother second time around. The daughter cannot and never could express her anger towards her own mother, and so she transfers it to her own child instead and physically abuses.

Stand-in abuse
A child who is closely related to one parent or resembles that parent may be abused by the other. It may represent a way of punishing the partner without undermining the marriage. The child, often a stepchild, becomes the 'whipping boy'. Children have an uncanny way of spotting the critical moment in a marital conflict. They then misbehave, attracting the joint anger of both parents. But by this method they have avoided the greater fear – that their parents might split up.

Closeness only after violence
Parents may have only experienced closeness with their own parents after episodes of violence. The pattern is repeated with their own children. Provocative behaviour produces punishment, and only then can the parents behave warmly. The children likewise learn that by their bad behaviour they will suffer punishment, but get the cuddles they so desperately want afterwards when the parents give love to assuage their guilt. This pattern describes how Lily responded to her child (p 20).

Transferred abuse
A child may represent to a parent a hated significant person or

event. The parent's irrational way of trying to blot out the individual or events is to attack the child. For the child this is doubly abusive. To be attacked because you are a symbol of something or somebody is particularly objectifying.

MOVING CIRCLES CONSTRUCT AGAIN

Let's now go right back to our moving circles construct and look at the neighbourhood, social and economic factors (circle 3).

Poverty is not in itself a cause of abuse, but the stress and lack of support and resources which characterize extreme social disadvantage can reduce the parents' general adaptation and self-control, thereby increasing the likelihood of family violence. If you have money you can mitigate the stress of bringing up children. You can employ a nanny or use the services of a boarding school. Affluent families can maintain their privacy by seeking private counselling and private medical care. In this way they are less likely to appear on a child protection register. O'Toole and Nalephac (1983) goes further and suggests that if a parent and the professional share similar characteristics, especially socio-economic status and income, the parent is less likely to be labelled 'abusive'. Any injuries sustained by the child will be diagnosed as accidental. The greater the social distance between client and worker the greater the danger of the label of abuse.

According to Krugman (1986) unemployment does not *cause* child abuse but there is a *relationship* between unemployment and physical abuse. In 1989 it was found that overall only 13 per cent of the mothers and 31 per cent of the fathers of the registered abused children 'were in paid employment' (Creighton and Noyes 1989). In fact poverty could be seen as one of the institutionalized forms of abuse. Rob Irvine (1988) suggests 'it is not possible to prove that poverty and its correlates cause child abuse but sufficient circumstantial evidence has been amassed to indicate that for many poor people it is an important factor.' There is both qualitative and quantitative evidence to suggest there is some link between poverty and abuse (Becker and MacPherson 1986). But it must be equally firmly stated that obviously not all poor people abuse their children.

Stress can be accentuated by living in a 'drained' environment. It is only in soap operas that people living in deprived neighbourhoods are all-supportive. If you live on the twelfth floor of a tower block, the lifts are broken and your neighbours are able to move out of the damp flats because they have only two children and the Council has difficulty in re-housing you because you have six, you don't mesh with the neighbourhood. You know there is no caring community out there. You shut your door as soon as it's dark for fear of mugging. Social isolation can play its part in child abuse (Gil 1970, 1975). However as Walker stated (Walker et al 1988) many of the sociological 'factors are found in abusive families but they don't sufficiently explain the problem'. They must been seen as part of all the other interacting and interlocking factors.

Let's look at our last circle – wider factors (4). Everyone is affected by the attitudes and philosophies that are around them. We are all a product of the child-rearing patterns in our family of origin. Workers therefore have to be particularly sensitive when dealing with people whose cultures and values are not the same as theirs. However it would be a mistake to take the stance of extreme relativism in which judgement of humane treatment of children is suspended in the name of cultural sensitivity or awareness.

Different cultures have different values. The white Anglo-Saxon worker sees isolating the newborn into a room on its own as good child-care (Korbin 1981). Other cultures would see this as a form of cruelty and allowing children to cry themselves to sleep for fear of spoiling the child as emotional abuse. The white ideal of stimulating the child, getting the child to question and challenge and to become independent could be seen by an Asian parent as individualism and being irresponsible. The family group would be seen as the most important entity.

Within the last circle must be seen the effects of important issues of racism and the powerlessness of women in a patriarchal society. Added to all this are the advertisements that continue to objectify women and children – making them into possessions. All these attitudes interrelate with the other circles in our construct. All this tinder box needs is the match. The trigger factor may come in the form of a battle over eating, toilet training or discipline. The match is lit – the child is battered.

WORKING WITH PHYSICALLY ABUSING FAMILIES

If you work with the victims of abuse you too will be victimized. This has been true across the ages from the time of Christ to Martin Luther King. Human beings cannot bear to face the pain. In ancient times the messenger who brought bad news was killed. Now we attack the interviewing skills of the professional and kill off his or her reputation.

The child abuse arena is totally irrational. Everyone knows about Maria Colwell, but who has heard of Emma Lockhart? Yet she died about the same time. The difference was that it was the neighbours who saw Emma die a slow lingering death. According to John Stroud (1974) 'What reporter is going to put neighbours into the dock of his front page?' In the case of Maria there was far more mileage; social workers were involved! Attitudes are only going to change imperceptibly slowly. Workers in the child abuse arena cannot waste time bemoaning this deep-rooted phenomenon. What we can do, is make our response as sharp as possible, be clear as to our role and demand good, structured supervision.

Authority

To cope successfully, every worker has to engage in a good deal of self-work around authority. If you work for a Social Service Department authority is delegated to you by your department under Section 47 and Section 17 of the Children Act 1989. The first of these Sections authorizes you to make such enquiries, considered necessary for you to decide if you have 'reasonable cause to suspect a child is suffering or is likely to suffer' any significant harm. The second demands you safeguard and promote the well-being of the child. Encouraged by government exhortation, all relevant agencies have drawn up internal procedures, and multi-disciplinary ones are agreed by local Area Child Protection Committees. All this gives the worker authority to intervene if there is abuse.

Authority has many faces. Blom Cooper in the Beckford Report (A Child in Trust 1985) stated 'Authority is not a dirty word.' If we want to help abusing families we must see all the faces of authority and use them constructively in our work. So often only the coercive side of authority is to the fore. Authority has other faces. There is the personal authority of the worker's own beliefs about protecting children's rights. These are perhaps best summed up in the United Nations Charter on the rights of the child (UNICEF 1989). Because children are 'especially vulnerable, essentially dependent and developing human beings ... They have particular rights amongst the most fundamental of which are the right to have their basic development needs provided for and the right to be protected from abuse' (Erooga and Masson 1990) – in all its manifestations.

Workers also have the authority given to them by their training and profession. It is this that will make a worker aim to be objective and go the extra mile when a member of the lay public would have retaliated or given up.

Authority is a necessary therapeutic tool when working with parents who physically abuse. Battering parents will 'lie and cheat' (A Child in Trust 1985) and we must be alert to parental ruses. Workers have to develop that professional ability to balance the outreach caring approach with the forensic style that enables them to be up-front and to confront. It is this unique combination of confrontation and concern that can bring about change.

Abusive parents often need someone to set boundaries. They are so full of violence and terrified they will explode, damaging self, children and the worker. They need the non-retaliatory authority of a professional who will not be washed away by all the powerful feelings. Above all they need a helper who can maintain his or her role and position, since in childhood, they had weak parents who would either collapse if challenged or brutally retaliate.

Clients also have their own authority. They can block the worker's attempts to help and have the right to face the full rigours of the law and a decision made by a judicial body. The middle ground cannot always be found. Partnerships with parents may have to give way to the welfare of the child being paramount.

In all this, the worker has the right to expect the support and the authority of their agency. This also includes adequate administrative backup and good quality supervision.

If your agency does not have statutory authority you still have professional authority. Skill is also required in knowing when the case should be referred to Social Services or the police.

ILSW approach

To work effectively in the field of child abuse the worker needs to integrate into one holistic approach the operation of the law and the skills of his/her social work profession – the Integration of Law and Social Work (ILSW).

It is quite dangerous to disassociate yourself from the statutory role of your agency, if you work for a local authority. You are visiting a family regularly, using all your social work skills. Child abuse occurs. The temptation then is to throw away your social work skills and just operate the law. It is more therapeutic and honest instead, in a situation when the child abuse could become an issue, to make it clear to your client both implicitly and by explanation, the true nature of your contract, to marry your social work skills and your legal responsibilities into one approach. This approach includes your statutory responsibilities and must be kept alive throughout the contract. The danger often lurks in cases that have continued for a long time. Then the contract can get blurred. (See Chapter 10.)

It is easiest at the start of a new investigation. Then you can make it clear what is your task. Often you need to state that you can't give reassurances until the investigation is completed. Quick reassurances that you're sure everything will be all right early in the process are both dangerous and dishonest. You may have to make it clear that you will need to consider, check out, get more information and return. Considerable skill may be required to work with the angry and hurt feelings of parents who have been wrongfully accused. No one likes being investigated.

As workers we must expect a whole range of feelings and ploys to divert us from our task. Parents can play the victim. We become genuinely sorry for them and lose sight of what has happened to the child. Another diversionary tactic is the angry demand to know 'who reported us'. Parents can intimidate and make us psychological hostages (see Chapter 6). Alternatively they can be charming and co-operative, covering up extreme violence and hostility (Shearer 1990).

Games

Unless we keep our role very clear, the games parents can play lead us a merry dance. 'I thought you were supposed to help me – now you're taking me to court.' 'If you had helped me more I wouldn't be in this mess.' At a time of scarce resources this one often goes right home! 'It would be a pity to destroy our good relationship, can't you overlook things just this once?'

The confidentiality game may be played unless it has been made clear early on that in child abuse situations we are part of an interdisciplinary team and information has to be shared on a need-to-know basis. 'I'll just tell *you* if you keep it a secret'. The worker who is trapped by this becomes totally impotent.

Doubts about the value of residential care, or the lack of the right foster homes, can seduce us away from the main task. This may be a particular problem when dealing with black children. The lack of black foster parents can lead us to neglect the protection of black children, while suffering from what has been called 'white liberal immobilization' (Stevenson 1986).

Games will be successful if we haven't come to terms with the following issues:

1. 'I've got too much work to do already.' This can lead to an unconscious wish not to discover trouble as it will create work.
2. 'All anonymous calls are malicious.' The reasons why a caller phones may be spurious, but the information may be absolutely accurate.
3. 'I don't want to get involved in messy untidy problems. I only want to do "positive" social work.' But the steps necessary to protect children can be messy (Davies et al 1985).
4. 'I don't want to confront. I want to be liked and play the role of Mr/Ms Nice Guy.'
5. Fear of the client can lead to unconscious collusion.
6. 'I don't want to go to court and have my appraisal of the situation challenged in cross examination. Let's just monitor the case!'
7. Fear of publicity – of seeing yourself appearing in the national tabloids, can lead to work that gets stuck. You become afraid of doing something, afraid of doing nothing.
8. The most important issue of all is facing the pain of the child and the parents. Child abuse work 'exposes the adult

to feeling memories of his own childhood agonies' (Wardle 1975).

Violence

The fear of violence can bedevil child abuse work. Managers need to create an atmosphere that is professional. It must be possible to admit to concerns and it should not be seen as a sign of weakness or failure to take another colleague or a police officer with you on a visit. In very violent situations it might be better to be accompanied regularly by the police rather than terminate the case to protect workers. If it is too dangerous for social workers to visit without a police officer present, there is a strong possibility that it is too dangerous for the children to remain in the home.

The whole subject of working with hostile and violent clients should figure more prominently on social work courses. A good starting point is in recognizing the pain, anguish and fear that are goading the client. If possible, the most successful approach is one of firm calmness. Fear is catching and escalates the situation. It is easy to start off on the wrong foot because we have become the receptacle of all the collective fear and panic of our colleagues at the child protection conference.

Many mistakes have been made because the possibility of violence towards workers has only been considered if it is a new case. Eighty-five per cent of attacks on workers 'were from old clients' (Rowett 1986). We become omnipotent with people we know. We become blasé: 'I know Mrs Brown. I'll be perfectly all right.' We don't see the early signs of trouble. Noting Kaplan and Wheeler's five stages (1983) might help us handle violent situations with more skill and sensitivity. People robbed of power over their lives not only become angry but destructive, in order to reclaim their power.

1 The trigger phase
According to Kaplan the escalation of violence begins when a client starts to move from their own baseline.

2 The escalation stage
It is during this phase that the worker can be most effective. The signs of this stage are the tightening of the body, hands and feet start to tap, we hear a clicking noise, because the mouth

has become dry. There is a general state of agitation. This is when the worker can divert the danger. 'You're obviously upset by discussing this now, let's return and talk about it later in the interview.' Individualizing can be helpful. It is always a dangerous sign when clients start to categorize and depersonalize. 'You officials...'. 'You lot...'. If possible, think of ways of giving power back to the client, create choices. 'What do *you* think you should do now?' A break for a cup of tea is often advisable.

3 The crisis stage
By this stage the client has lost most of their rationality. It is no good appealing to their reason. Just get out. Broken chairs mend, broken bodies don't. In a white person a red face may indicate that the violence has blown. The most dangerous is the individual whose face is getting whiter and the voice quieter. With a black client the dilation of the eyes and the set of the face may give the clue.

4 The recovery stage
This can last as long as 90 minutes. Adrenalin once aroused to a significant level can last as an active agent for that period of time. Sometimes workers make the mistake of starting up the interview again too soon, re-igniting the embers of anger. Reassuring the client of their own safety can often foster the return to the baseline. Mental and physical exhaustion of the client actually leads to a return to a stage below his/her usual baseline and is called the post-crisis depression stage.

5 Post-crisis depression stage
This is the time when the clients become remorseful, tearful and shamefaced. At this point they can be more receptive to intervention efforts.

DAZPOE
Investigatory social work is a highly skilled process but is often not given the professional status it deserves. A mnemonic may help: DAZPOE. It is such an unusual word that it may be easily recalled at a time of crisis when everything is crashing about one's ears.

D is for data
The asking of questions to find out what went wrong is a way of showing concern and the beginning of the process which can put things right. The collection of data is the baseline for any work. A very useful guide is the Department of Health's *Protecting Children*, supplemented by the guidelines shown in the Appendix. So, building on the DoH guide (DoH 1988) the following are the areas where information needs to be gathered:

1. *The causes of concern*
2. *The child* Name. Age. Date of birth.
   - What are the parents' perceptions of the child and what has happened?
   - What are the child's perceptions?
   - What is the nature of the routine care given to the child?
   - Child's early history including medical, social, intellectual, educational, psychological developmental aspects – present state.
   - Social worker's perceptions.
3. *Family composition* Names. Ages. Dates of birth. Aliases.
4. *Individual profile of each parent and/or carer*
   - History: medical, social, psychological, intellectual, economic.
   - History of couple's and present relationships.
   - How do they individually and jointly relate to the community?
   - Family – power – communication – work – patterns.
   - What are the networks?
   - What other agencies are involved?
   - How have parents responded to help in the past?
5. *Physical conditions*
   - Housing.
6. *Finances*
   - Who handles the money?
7. *What needs to change*
   - In what period of time?
8. *How does this family handle stress?*
9. *How does this family solve problems?*

10 *Buoys*
    • What will help to keep this family afloat?
11 *Sharks*
    • What is likely to sabotage attempts to help?
12 *Alternatives*
    • What alternative sources of help are available?

Obviously not all the above information can be obtained on the first visit. Data collection is a process that should continue until the case is closed.

Data and referrals may come from a number of sources:

- *Anonymous* It is very easy to be prejudiced against anonymous referrers, who are not willing openly to acknowledge their concern. However it is dangerous not to take anonymous referrals very seriously.
- *Family members* Family members can refer cases for all the wrong reasons; the referral may nevertheless be absolutely valid.
- *Liars* Liars can also tell the truth.
- *Neighbours* As far back as the Colwell Report (1974) concern was expressed that agencies were not user-friendly. To wait in a long queue in dingy offices without privacy is not conducive to parent or neighbour sharing their concerns.
- *Professionals* Information from professionals can be just as problematic as from the lay public. Referrals can often be woolly. Colleagues may have to be given time to talk about a problem before it is possible to see if a referral should be made. What is everyday work for a social worker may be extremely anxiety-provoking for a nursery nurse.

Sometimes professionals want a matter put right without any hassle or the preliminaries of an investigation. They may want the social service worker to wave a magic wand and put it right, without even telling the parents a referral has been made. Honesty from the beginning usually means the matter can be handled more effectively. The social worker should negotiate. Is the referrer going to tell the parents or shall the social worker?

Anxiety can do strange things to colleagues. This is what explains why a worker hangs on to anxious information about a child till 4.30 on a Friday afternoon or the last day of term. This sort of referral feels like a 'dumping' exercise to the social worker involved, creating anger and vitiating the whole process.

It is important that workers are clear as to whether data is fact, observation, interpretation or rumour. In the Carly Taylor, Darren Clarke, and Max Piazzani cases data was seen as exaggerated and treated as idle gossip and therefore not valued (DHSS 1982).

Children are often not listened to. Darren Clarke said 'Charlie had done it.' Wayne Brewer said 'Daddy did it.' Maria said she would like to live on a farm. 'No-one would be able to find me there' (DHSS 1982). Adults in the Darren Clarke case gave information in such a flat way it was discounted.

Abusing parents, because they feel so empty, will defend themselves by making workers feel particularly intrusive. This is where supervisors may have to use their authority and demand that workers go back and complete their investigation.

An investigation is the beginning of the therapeutic process. Workers must combine their investigatory skills with their social work skills and insight. Joint work with the police is therefore part of the process. An investigation requires workers to find out Who? Where? What? When? How? and Why? Some insight into *why* is particularly important to facilitate the next stage of treatment.

In the case of Terry, there was no doubt that the father had pushed his son's fingers into some white hot metal in his workshop.

It was however crucial for the success of further work with the family that all the parties involved had some sort of understanding *why*. His wife (the boy's stepmother) had been goading him all morning that he loved his son more than he did her. The boy, in misguided loyalty to his own mother, couldn't relate to his stepmother, though he desperately wanted to. He constantly tried to break up the new marriage. The father's primitive response was reprehensible but understandable. All parties needed to gain some understanding at the investigatory stage, not months later when the case was allocated to a permanent worker.

A is for assessment
I once heard a colleague describe assessment as the mulling

over and evaluation of each piece of information. Then comes the application of professional knowledge and judgement to all the known facts: seeing if patterns or themes emerge that will give an overall understanding. Assessment means processing facts into appropriate action, using the data collected. So often anxious workers cope with their anxiety by just getting more and more information, skipping the assessment stage and launching straight into planning.

Part of the function of assessment is the evaluation of risk. Often the word risk is wrongly used. The event has occurred. The child has already been abused. What has to be assessed is whether the child will be re-abused.

It is a good idea to fine tune the word *risk*. There are here-and-now risks. Mary has a broken leg, we must act *now*. If Peter is neglected we are looking at cumulative risk. That is, a single incident by itself may not constitute a risk. The question in these circumstances is *when* should the worker act? Lastly there are potential risks. *What* would make us act? Mrs Brown is mentally ill. What would need to happen for her child to be at risk?

A great deal of time has been spent in criminal studies assessing dangerousness. Many words have been written about dangerous families (Dale 1986). The trouble is that predictions have often led to an alarming range of error, between 54 per cent and 99 per cent according to Monahan and Cummings (1975). Predictions also offer no indication as to which of the many potential abusers will abuse. Checklists often relate to individuals and overlook changing dynamic situations. One violent boyfriend leaves, only to be replaced by another. If certain features are not found within a family it can lead to complacency on behalf of the workers.

Personally I don't like the word predictors. To make it clear we are not being scientific, I prefer the term 'losing cards'. One losing card by itself is no indication at all, but if a case has a large number of losing cards then it would be good practice to demand regular supervision on that case. Then, forget the losing cards, and focus on the dynamics of the case and what the clients and their behaviour are telling us about the welfare of the child.

With that government health warning as it were, the following losing cards 'test' can be used as a rough guide

(Greenland 1987, Kotelchuk 1982, Murphy et al 1985, Orkow 1985, Schmitt 1978, Smith and Hanson 1980).

The terrible thirteens
1. Original abuse was sadistic.
2. Poor parenting skills – can't cope with crying – child underweight.
3. Poor parent/child interaction.
4. Family stress (even good news can be stressful – like pregnancy or the birth of a child) – or the stress of chronic illness.
5. Too high expectations of a child's milestones.
6. Parents who can't control their anger.
7. Social isolation.
8. Substance abuse.
9. Parents young (under 24).
10. One partner not the parent.
11. Low IQ.
12. Partners who were abused themselves.
13. Previous abuse.

Z is for zoom in
The worker needs to zoom in on what needs to be changed and where the work has to be targetted. Each abusing family is unique but the following areas are often the most productive.

- Child management skills – working with parents *and* child.
- Building up self-esteem.
- Developing social skills.
- Work with anger control.
- Work with stress.
- Network building to combat social isolation.
- Improving problem-solving strategies.
- Work with situational factors such as poor housing and unemployment.

The worker must have a 'time plan' for the 'zoom in' programme. If the child is a baby, work around feeding, bathing and dressing would be a priority to be achieved quickly. Any programme must include clarity about who in the interdisciplinary team does what with whom, with a note about what skills are required.

Conflict is not always negative. A family may need two

workers using conflicting approaches, but it has to be planned and accepted conflict. Differences of perception can be acceptable but not so as to destroy the whole of the interdisciplinary approach.

The key worker needs to have a systematic approach so that recognition, investigation, assessment, planning, implementation, rehabilitation or separation and finally disengagement (DoH 1988) are followed through by the whole team where appropriate.

Families should not have to fit into any particular social work methods. The method should be made to fit the family.

P is for child protection plan
The plan should be created and carried through with enthusiasm, based on the resources that actually exist. It is no use looking back and bewailing lack of resources or lost opportunities. Every effort must be made as a team to help the plan succeed. The plans must be shared with professionals, parents and where appropriate the child. Commitment by all concerned is essential for success.

O is for operation of the plan
Be courageous. If the plan isn't working renegotiate a new one. Always remember that Jasmine Beckford's fate was probably sealed when the new information about her putting on weight when in care and losing it at home was not listened to. It's easy to get stuck with the plans drawn up first by the child protection conference. Just more of the same is often not the answer. A totally new plan may have to be initiated.

E is for evaluation
Evaluation is what prevents 'drift'. We all need something to check our work against. This is where our friend DAZPOE comes in useful. What new data do we need? What is the data telling us and does it affect our assessment? Are we zooming down on the right areas of work? Is our plan still valid? Have we lost steam in its operation? What success are we having? Continuous evaluation keeps us on our toes. Nothing less is essential when dealing with life/death issues.

3 Children in the Shadows – Marital Violence

Marital violence was once 'thought of as either a family secret or acceptable behaviour within a patriarchal society' (Jaffe et al 1990). The trouble is that having discovered the phenomenon of the battered wife we are so transfixed by the destructive potential of the terrifying violence between the adults that it is almost impossible to look at the effects it has upon the children. The spotlight beamed on physical and sexual abuse has made the darkness even murkier for other faces of child abuse. Children caught up in marital violence are still very much in the shadows.

Uncovering the facts is shattering. If we want to prevent wife battering we have to start with the child witness. Violence observed at home in childhood is repeated later in life. Straus et al (1980) went so far as to state that sons who witness their father's violence have a 1000 per cent greater likelihood of violence against their own partners than sons who do not. Yet obviously not all sons who grow up in violent homes become batterers.

Retrospective accounts from women in battered wives shelters reveal as many as 80 per cent recall witnessing their mother being assaulted by their father (Gayford 1975). Extreme events can stay with children and affect them for a lifetime. The tragedy is the effects can be inter-generational. As one worker in a shelter exclaimed 'What really gets me down is seeing the daughters of women we sheltered and counselled ten years ago coming to us as battered wives ... Their daughters are repeating the pattern' (Macleod 1987).

HOW CHILDREN LEARN

Children caught up in conjugal violence learn in conflicting ways. They hide under the duvet to muffle the sounds of angry voices but at the same time strain to hear what is said. They may be actual witnesses to the violence or see the results next morning. Even worse, they may experience seeing their mother abused by a whole string of male partners.

Both parents tend to minimize or deny the presence of children during violent episodes. Rosenberg (1984) found that children had seen and heard many more episodes than the adults realized. Leighton (1989) indicates that in 68 per cent of cases of wife abuse the children are present.

BAD LESSONS

Conflict resolution
Violence between parents teaches children so many bad lessons. Children learn that violence is an appropriate form of conflict resolution which has a place within family interaction. Violence is learned as the basis of power and control in the family. Children may be asked to watch their mothers' victimization as a lesson in patriarchal control, to learn what may happen to them if they disobey their fathers (Finkelhor et al 1983).

Sexism
Wife-abusing families are a breeding ground for sexism. Inequality of power, inequality in decision-making and rigid sex roles are encouraged. Love means possession, while disagreement is equated with hostility. Authority and discipline are interpreted to mean the right to control by force. The idea of negotiation is rejected as a sign of the loss of authority or weakness. Expression of feelings signifies weakness (Elbow 1982). To go further: what children come to realize is that even if someone outside the family, professional or otherwise, gets

to hear about what goes on, sadly no preventive action is likely to be taken (Wilson et al 1989).

Interactional feedback
The lessons learnt are not as simple as direct cause and effect. There tends to be an interactional feedback. If the children want or need something, or fail to meet parental expectations they become the focus of the next parental battle. The children then take on an exaggerated sense of responsibility. They feel they caused the violence and were the authors of the parents' fate. In turn they feel that they should be able to prevent the violence by defusing their father's anger and protecting their mother. If they could be perfect, peace would reign.

Mistrust
At the peak of the violence the mother is least able to protect or support. The worse the violence, the more her sense of helplessness and hopelessness increases. Fostered by the batterer, the mother's feelings of isolation and poor self-esteem mean she 'underestimates the lethality of her relationship for herself or her children' (Browne 1987). Economic and social factors keep her imprisoned within her own home. Depressed and anxious she has no energy left to support or give understanding to her children. So the basic lesson of trust is not learnt. The children cannot trust her.

Lack of autonomy
Children in violent homes cannot gradually and appropriately learn about autonomy. The adults around them cannot control themselves. How then can they limit and set boundaries for the children? This leaves the children vulnerable to frightening internal impulses. They may push for parental limits to be set. This leads to the abuser accusing the mother of inadequate parenting which in turn becomes the focal point for yet more violence. The children learn that men are not personally responsible for their behaviour, rather that the victims, their mothers, brought the violence on by their own behaviour or just by being women. So the very persons on whom the children depend for safety and nurture can offer neither – the basic necessities for any human trying to become their own person.

Secrecy

The family locked in domestic violence is often isolated from the community. The child experiences family members as isolated from one another (Cantoni 1981). Yet at the same time the children are expected to feel close. The symbiotic bond of the violent marriage keeps the child from learning the natural lesson of how to grow away from the family unit. All they do learn is that the violence must be 'kept a secret'. To talk could lead to punishment from the abuser and shame within the wider network.

THE YO-YO SYNDROME

Research by the NSPCC has made a key contribution towards drawing professional attention to the plight of children caught in marital conflict (Moore 1975a, 1975b and Moore et al 1981). The research uncovered nine main outcomes.

(i) The first gave its name to the study – the yo-yo syndrome – and was one grandmother's graphic attempt to describe the pattern of violence. If you can remember playing with a yo-yo it goes down its own string, remains still for a few split seconds before it climbs back up its own string. The process is repeated again and again. Marital violence seems to have the same pattern: violence, then inexplicable silence, then violence again. Couples accuse each other of real or extra-marital relationships; or there are rows over children, food or sex. The couples seem to have an unerring ability to spot when the violence could turn lethal. One of the partners departs, leaving at least one child within the marital home as a return ticket. After a day, a week or a month, the couple will reunite as if yoked together in violence. The violence of couples in the main does not seem to result from a deliberate aim to kill the partner, as noted by Faulk (1974).

(ii) Eighty per cent of the children in the study were adversely affected by the violence. The words most often used by the researchers to describe the children were 'jumpy', 'anxious', 'nervy'. The damage can begin before birth. The male abuser, before pregnancy, aims for the face, arms and legs. When the woman is pregnant he aims for the stomach: a form of pre-birth battering.

(iii) The most obvious effect was the scapegoating. The child most favoured by one partner was often rejected, physically or emotionally, by the other. One father in a study confessed he couldn't stand his son as his voice was just like that of his wife. 'He even repeats her very words!'

(iv) Then there were children who turned themselves into containers, who tried to hold the violence within themselves. This often led to somatic conditions. One boy in the study, aged four, had eczema which always became worse at the peak of his parents' violence. Another younger child literally tried to hold his breath as a symbolic way of freezing the violent situation. There were numerous incidents of soiling, speech defects and failure to thrive.

(v) Many of the children put themselves into the role of mediator, trying to forestall the parents' violence. The children's attempts usually failed. It was a double failure. Violence was not forestalled and parents then attacked them. One six-year-old kept a bizarre notebook bought from a superstore. He noted down meticulously the visits from the police and the personal services, believing such a record would serve to protect his family from their own violence. It did not.

(vi) A significant number of children had school problems. Those in the study were often too tired to attend school after the drama of the previous night. Some children truanted while others sat at the desk but were emotionally absent. Others broke into unexplained bouts of unprovoked violence having previously been quiet and unobtrusive. Many of the children, not surprisingly, were underachievers. Some of this was undoubtedly due to the amount of geographical and emotional movement in which they were involved.

(vii) The most damaged group were those used as pawns. Parents, though they denied it, only saw the children as pawns in their parental battles, and not as people in their own right. One mother left after a bout of violence. The father threatened to retaliate by pouring petrol over himself and the child – and lighting it. As he had done something similar a few weeks previously, the mother returned to the violent partnership. What does it mean to be the instrument for getting your mother beaten again?

(viii) Children can cope with the violence surrounding them by becoming violent themselves. A three-year-old after a violent incident between his parents became 'difficult' to manage, aggressive and disobedient. He would hit his mother and said 'daddy smacks mummy because she has been naughty.' For the mother this is a double blow. Already a victim of her husband's violence, now the child attacks her too.

(ix) Children can get accidentally injured in the parental violence. A mother may pick up the baby, perhaps unconsciously using the child as a screen. Nigel aged six was hit by a knife aimed at his father. A particularly vulnerable time is when one parent leaves the home. All the violence and hurt which has been contained between the parents can then be turned on the children. Having lost one parent to be injured by the remaining one is a double emotional blow.

UP DATING

Compared with other faces of child abuse, for instance physical and sexual, there have not been as many studies of the effects of marital conflict since the publication of the Yo-Yo Report. The children involved could well become forgotten again.

Of the studies which have been undertaken, Levine (1975) discovered that children involved in conjugal violence displayed anxiety and conduct disorders. Hilberman and Munson (1977) reported that children involved in violent families had school problems. 'Conduct problems were more frequently reported for males and somatic and internalizing problems were more in evidence for females.' Westra and Martin (1981) state that children of conjugal violence show an inordinate number of physical problems including difficulty in hearing and poor articulation. They add 'More aggressive behaviour was noted including lower verbal cognitive and motor abilities.' Pfouts (1982) confirms the acting out of children. Forsstrom-Cohen and Rosenbaum (1985) state that exposure to marital violence is associated with high levels of anxiety for *both* girls and boys. Wolfe in 1986 found that the children showed lower social competence.

GENDER ISSUES

What is interesting and complex are some of the gender issues. As Elbow (1982) states, the children in violent families have terrible identity problems. They do not want to identify 'with the violence of the abuser or the hopelessness of the victim.' The children begin to equate maleness with hurting women and femaleness with being hurt by men. So some children struggle with this unacceptable and confusing self-image by becoming aggressive. Some boys will avoid identification with their father's aggressive behaviour by denying the violence and idealizing and exaggerating his positive characteristics.

Hughes (1982) showed how boys of six to eleven years identified strongly with their fathers. Sopp-Gilson (1980) and Wolfe et al (1986) describe how boys in other studies mimicked the male model and became aggressive towards their mothers, female staff and peers. In yet another study, girls as they reached adolescence developed an extreme distrust of men and expressed negative attitudes about marriage (Hughes 1986). The saddest thing is that as they begin dating, the girls of violent marriages are more likely to become the victims of physical violence from boyfriends. They tend to see such behaviour as inevitable or an indicator of love. De Lang (1986) observed that children in shelters were often socially isolated from their peers and did not relate to the activities or interests of those in their age group. She estimated that approximately 40 per cent of these children had problems interacting with other children and adults. Hinchey and Gavelek (1982) found that children from violent homes exhibited a deficiency in their capacity to recognize the emotional state of the 'social other'. Such a deficiency may thus inhibit the development of intimate relationships.

FOCUS ON THE CHILDREN

Successful techniques have been discovered to help warring and violent parents (Moore et al 1981) and a great deal has been written about understanding marital conflict in general. However apart from work undertaken with children of divorcing parents, not much attention has been given to helping children who continue to live in situations where there is conjugal violence. As children in such homes tend to be isolated from their peers, working in groups is particularly effective. But a great deal has been achieved by face-to-face work.

To begin with, the children need help in discussing the confusion and conflict surrounding their feelings of anger, fear, sadness and shame. This can be done by 'labelling'. Happy, sad, angry and frightened faces are drawn and then talked about. In a variation of this game, each child has a label taped on their back representing a feeling. All the other children in the group then have to mime non-verbally that feeling to the child. When the child has guessed correctly another child becomes 'it' in the game. What has to be established is that it is perfectly appropriate to have feelings, but ways have to be discovered of how to express these feelings that are not damaging to the self or others.

More than anything else it is important to emphasize that in no way is the child to blame for the parents' fighting. Parental actions must be seen and clearly identified as adult issues and not the responsibility of the child. Children need to be helped to discover ways of keeping safe and who they can turn to or ring if the violence becomes too destructive. A formal list of emergency telephone numbers and addresses often helps. Because children caught up in families where there is domestic violence do not bring friends home, their social contacts are often very restricted. The worker or the group may need to help the child discover who could be supportive and willing to listen, when they are feeling sad or frightened.

Living day in and day out with family violence can produce a severe lack of self-confidence and esteem (Cantoni 1981; Hinchey et al 1982). The game of 'self inventory' can be helpful. A piece of paper is folded. Inside the child makes a collage of how they feel about themselves. On the outside they make another collage to describe how they think others feel about them. The group or, in individual sessions, the worker then reinforce these perceptions, adding positive attitudes and refuting negative ones.

Children need to be given some understanding of violence within families; to de-bunk some of the myths they have taken in as truths, such as, the mother was solely to blame, or their father's violence was caused totally by alcohol or work stress. Particularly confusing is the cycle of violence. At one moment separation appears inevitable, reconciliation totally obvious the next.

Honestly looking at the home situation can have elements of reassurance about it for the child. Discussing what could happen and considering the possibility of divorce or separation of their parents and looking at the positive aspects of the present situation highlights the choices that could be available. Perhaps with the assistance of lawyers, workers should evaluate more often the possibility of removing children from homes when they are being emotionally damaged by the violence.

Work with the children obviously has to be meshed with the general work with the parents. Children also have to be given permission to talk about things they have kept secret for so long. Jaffe (1990) discovered that 88 per cent of mothers reported the children as enjoying the groups. They also found a positive improvement in the children's behaviour. Further, the groups allowed the children to separate their feelings of love for their fathers without having to accept his violent behaviour. The Home Office (Smith 1989) considered the possibility of 'half a million married women' as the 'victims of domestic violence each year'. As many of these women will have children, there are very large numbers of children in the shadows who desperately need help, not just in their own right but to protect future generations.

4 Tabloid Turbulence – Sexual Abuse

After years of aversion gaze, the tabloid press have suddenly discovered child sexual abuse and have now over-sensationalized a complex and painful subject. One good thing to come out of all this attention is that the problem is now out of the closet. We have made progress in the arena of disclosure and assessment but therapeutic work with the child, family and perpetrator lags far behind. Disclosure without therapy is a second rape of the child.

MYTHS

In spite of all the radio and television programmes the lay public, and not only the lay public, want to hang on to the myth that the typical sex-abuser is the dirty old man in a raincoat lurking in a public park to pick up children. The reality is quite different. The sexual abuser is usually known to the child. Sexual abusers are fathers, stepfathers, mothers' boyfriends, neighbours, adolescent babysitters and even mothers.

It may help to get some of the other myths out of the way. First, many offenders are individuals whose primary sexual orientation is not towards children. Nor is sexual abuse often a one-off event. In many of the cases the continuum of sexual contact between the child and the adult extends over a period of time. In one study 232 child molesters admitted to having over 17,000 victims (Abel et al 1987).

Sexual abuse is not confined to nubile daughters and their fathers. It can occur at birth and continue throughout a whole lifetime. A competent professional at a course I ran recently admitted her father had sexually abused her until she was 36 years old. Children can leave the household, marry, have their own children and still be lured back into the sexually abusing set-up.

Because the family keeps the big secret, professionals working with families may never know. As Kempe and Kempe (1978) said

> A discussion of incest and other forms of sexual abuse of children is likely to bring forth strong feelings of revulsion and disbelief ... but these are the same feelings that have caused professionals to shy away from the problems of sexual abuse and to underestimate the severity and extent.

Another myth that stalks the law courts is that the child will tell the mother. Sexually abused children rarely tell. After all, the child has been told to keep the abuse a secret and abuse happens only when the child is alone with the perpetrator. As the perpetrator is likely to be a trusted adult the child does not know how to cope with the feelings aroused and is entirely dependent on that adult for an interpretation of the experience. The child has to believe the self-protective story of the adult. 'It's a secret.' 'You mustn't tell your mother, it would kill her.' 'If you do tell it will break up the family.' The trouble with this last statement is so often it turns out to be true. So the secrecy of the act is both bad and dangerous but the secrecy is also a source of fear and a promise of safety. 'Everything will be all right if you don't tell.'

The secret can take on a monstrous magical quality. If the child does tell, the secret becomes even more powerful. Adults can collude in a conspiracy of silence. And even when professionals know, nothing happens. 'There's not enough evidence.' The non-abusing parent may make it obvious, consciously or unconsciously, she doesn't want to know. She might make comments like 'Nice grandad, he wouldn't do such things – you have a filthy mind.' Alternatively the adults may become hysterical – the child may be blamed – 'You led him on.' If the child is removed, the siblings will blame the victim for being in care. It's not therefore surprising that children retract and then face the double jeopardy of being proved a liar.

Child sexual abuse is not a romantic Lolita-like situation but means waking up to find your body is being explored, or finding a penis filling your mouth. As one four-year-old confided to his social worker, he could tell the difference between his stepfather, stepuncle and stepgrandfather, when they came to him in the middle of the night, by the different tastes of their penises. So abused children do not run away, but feign sleep and move silently to another part of the bed. They learn survival tactics that may be the prelude to a lifetime of self-destructive behaviour.

Another myth is that there has been for all time an incest taboo. Yet we know Cleopatra married her brother and they were both from a long line of royal incestuous marriages. In Egyptian culture at that time, inheritance went through the female line and incest was thus a way of keeping the family fortune intact (Murray 1963). I am reliably informed that in the time of Pope Leo III, no marriages were allowed closer than the seventh degree and even godparents were later drawn into the incest taboo.

The most telling argument for me is that children are too young, vulnerable, inexperienced socially, emotionally and economically to give consent to sex. What is more, it deprives the child of the most important gift of all, a normal parent/child relationship. Child sexual abuse is an exploitation of power which disrupts the developmental tasks of childhood. As child sexual abuse is not an easy subject to cope with, particularly in a world where there is uncertainty as to what degree of sexual contact is abusive, some definition may be of help.

DEFINITIONS

One of the most widely accepted definitions is that of Schechter and Roberge (1976): 'The involvement of dependent, developmentally immature children and adolescents in sexual activities that they do not fully comprehend, are unable to give informed consent to, and that violate the social taboos of family roles.' Added to this should be Brant and Tisza's (1977) additional comment: 'Exposure of children in sexual stimulation inappropriate to the child's age and level of psycho-social development.' Feminists Hall and Lloyd (1989) suggest any definition should include:

> The betrayal of trust and responsibility.
> The abuse of power.
> The inability of children to consent.
> An indication of the wide range of sexual activity.
> The use of force or threats. The child's perception of the threat even if the abuse is non-coercive threatening or non-violent.

They feel Sgroi (1982) gets the nearest with

> Child sexual abuse is a sexual act imposed on a child who lacks the emotional maturational and cognitive development. The ability to lure a child into a sexual relationship is based on the all-powerful and dominant position of the adult or older perpetrator which is in sharp contrast with the child's age, dependence or subordinate position. Authority and power enable the perpetrator implicitly or directly, to coerce the child into sexual compliance.

The only quarrel I have with this is the reference to age. Recently my advice was sought in a case in which the perpetrator was a child of five who was sexually abusing a child of seven. The facts demonstrated that it was definitely not childhood sexual exploration.

Child sexual abuse is more than simple sexual penetration and can perhaps be divided under three headings.

No physical contact
There may be no touching, but displaying of breasts, penis, vagina, anus; masturbating while the child watches; having intercourse while the child watches; undressing seductively in front of the child; using adult nudity to stimulate or shock the child; watching a child while he/she uses the toilet or undresses, all to get sexual stimulation.

Often parents will challenge a worker about such behaviour as not being against the law. The best thing is to avoid an argument as this behaviour is difficult to prove. Instead the worker should stand firmly on the statement that such behaviour is poor child-care.

Touching
This may involve kissing the child intimately (there is a big difference between a fatherly peck and exploring with the tongue the inside of the child's mouth); fondling the child's breasts, belly, buttocks; requiring the child to fondle the adult; masturbating the child or requiring the child to masturbate the adult; rubbing adult sexual parts against the child's body.

Intrusion
In this situation, oral or genital contact between the child and the adult is initiated: requiring the child to fellate (oral contact with the penis); to perform cunnilingus (oral contact with the vagina) or analingus (oral contact with the anus); placing the penis between the child's thighs; penetrating the child's anus, vagina using fingers, object or penis.

WHY SEXUAL ABUSE?

The trouble with so much of the research is that clients in penal institutions have been used as the sample. The difficulty with child sexual abuse is that most offences do not come to the notice of professionals. If the perpetrator totally denies the offence, the case may not get to court. Many cases which do reach court are then not proved. So those in prison are an unrepresentative sample. However David Finkelhor and his associates (1986) have brought together in a masterly way all the current research to answer the question 'Why?' They have used four headings:

> *emotional congruence* – where there is a fit between the adult's emotional needs and the characteristics of the children;
> *sexual arousal* – why people find children sexually arousing;
> *blockage* – why individuals are blocked in their ability to meet their sexual and emotional needs in adult relationships;
> *disinhibition* – why conventional inhibitions against having sex with children are overcome.

Indicators
It may be helpful to look at some indicators, but this is no easy

matter. Unlike physical abuse often there are no medical signs. The child may say 'Dad's not the same as he used to be.' He may not be. His leg may be in plaster. But what the child might be trying to convey is that the relationship has become a sexual one.

A sudden change of mood and regressive behaviour such as wetting the bed may be a clue. The eneuresis may be caused by a whole range of problems. A fear of men, sleep disturbances, nightmares and non-organic tummy aches may be the first signs of trouble. These should be carefully followed to see if they are significant. Depression and withdrawal into a world of his or her own may be important, as is a child who appears pseudo-mature. If all the children at school are swanking about their 'puppy dog' relationships with boys, the child who is sleeping with her father is bound to look down her nose.

The causes of sexually transmitted diseases in children should always be investigated as should excessive masturbation and sexually provocative behaviour (TUFTS 1984). The sad thing is that abused children do not know the difference between affection and sexual behaviour. Thus their behaviour can subject them to further abuse. Not all children with nappy rash are sexually abused, but constant soreness in the genital area and micturition with pain should be explored. We have also learnt that children who run away are not always running to something but may be running *away* – from sexual abuse (McCormack et al 1986).

THE SLIPPERY SLOPE

Trying not to fall into the trap of making a very complex subject too simple but acknowledging that this book is meant to be a primer, the construct of the *slippery slope* may be valuable (Chesterman 1985, Summit and Kryso 1978). There has been a tendency to lump together all sexual abusers as being the same. They are not a homogeneous group. Therapeutic measures which are used to help perpetrators described as 'at the top of the slope' will be entirely invalid for clients who would be placed nearer 'the bottom of the slope'. Professional carers therefore have to face the fact that they may be unable to offer any help to change the behaviour of some perpetrators. This has considerable wider implications when trying to protect children.

Before looking at the slippery slope in detail one has to put sexual abuse into a wider context. All sexual abuse is an abuse of power and the feminist analysis sees

> 'the problem of masculinity' at the centre of child abuse. It asserts we live in a patriarchal society which is reinforced by the social structure of the family with father as the powerholder, mother as the nurturer and children as dependent. Male power is also held responsible for the silence surrounding sexual abuse as mothers and children have no power to break the silence. They need to maintain the family identity to prevent a revelation of the truth since to tell would risk isolation (Hall and Lloyd 1989).

At the beginning of the slope would be parents who encourage and stimulate over-dependence of the child on the adult. They strike up inappropriate emotional attachments that bind the child to the parent. The child when adult may leave the nest, but remain more wedded to the parent than their partner. This could be called *emotional sexual abuse* and is our first signpost.

Then follows *vicarious sexual abuse*. Parents, under the guise of affection, indulge in lingual kissing. Other perpetrators hide behind doors to watch the child undressing. Faller (1988) tells of a cohabitee who took the bathroom door off so he could watch the two daughters aged 11 and 13 going to the toilet.

Our next signpost reads *ideological sexual abuse*. Parents may fear their sexual hangups have been caused by a too rigid and oppressive upbringing. So when their child arrives they are determined not to make the same mistake. One mother on a school's educational programme confided to the lecturer that her boy aged six was trying to have intercourse with a child of similar age. Her story unfolded. Her husband read a 'soft porn' magazine so it was left on a coffee table. She believed, rightly, the body was beautiful, so she bathed with the child. As the story continued it was quite clear, this little boy was being stimulated too quickly too soon.

The next signpost covers a very small group of *psychotic patients* who mesh the child into their sick fantasies. One very sick cohabitee said the child concerned was God and the only way to stop the four-year-old losing her powers was to have sex with her.

To get back to our slippery slope. On the next signpost is *endogamous incest*. We are looking at a damaging distortion of family relationships but this in no way takes the major responsibility from the male. To save complexity, as 90 per cent of the perpetrators are men (see p 73), the male pronoun will be used to refer to perpetrators.

The perpetrator is not noticeably impulsive and may appear to the outside world to be well adjusted and well functioning. However, the father is flying from adult realities. The couple are becoming more and more frustrated with each other (maybe for good reasons) and the man turns to the child. In this category the perpetrator is hungering for closeness and a sense of belonging he seldom experienced as a child. The sexual abuse is more an attempt to get minimal basic nurturance than sex. This character often moves into a family where there are already children. He becomes more and more frightened he will be discovered and in his mind his partner becomes the punishing mother he once had.

What may have started gently becomes more and more coercive. 'If you don't come with me I shall have to start with the younger ones.' The child who therefore sacrifices him or herself then finds out later he was having sex with the younger children all the time: a double betrayal.

All the usual excuses are used. 'The child seduced me!' 'I was just preparing her for marriage – better I do it than a clumsy adolescent.' But, when found out, this category of perpetrator becomes acutely depressed and will genuinely promise anything to get back to the family. He cannot function outside of his family. This has significance for the helping process.

A DETOUR

The mother

Many mothers do *not* know that sexual abuse is taking place. They may be depressed, feeling the loss of their girlhood attraction and may even resent their children. They may delegate chores to the children because they have to work and therefore the relationship between child and father gradually changes. Other women are often totally dependent on their male partner both emotionally and financially.

The mother is therefore in an impossible position. She loves or needs the partner and doesn't want to believe what is happening. If the mother does open up and tell, peculiar things happen. The family is disgraced, and has to face life on state benefits. The mother is blamed. Her femininity is criticized: 'Why did he have to turn to the children?' Sometimes the only way to survive is to use the major psychological mechanism of coping by way of denial.

It *is* possible in sexually abusing families to keep the secret because of the denial and communication patterns and the grooming process that may have started when the child was very young, long before the abuse began.

GROOMING (Christiansen and Reid 1990)

The perpetrator consciously and unconsciously isolates the child. Communications from the child are trivialized and distorted: 'Oh no one believes Mary, she makes up so many stories.' Everyone is made dependent on the perpetrator. He encourages splits and punishes any dependence on anyone except himself. He builds up trust with the child by buying presents and spending time with the child. He says that anything daddy does is right and he would never do anything to hurt the child. He makes the child a *favourite*, making it clear he expects favours back. The child feels special and role boundaries become blurred. The father hints he is lonely, and the child must become his 'special' friend.

This all *alienates* the child from the mother and peers who could later become a possible source of support and help. The child becomes totally dependent upon the father. 'Daddy's games are much more interesting and he's a better friend!'

A stifling relationship of *secrecy* begins: 'Mother doesn't understand me.' The first signs of fear may begin to enter into the dyad, in response to any comment made about the relationship or attempts to break it up.

Boundary violations begin: the father baths the child; there is joint bathing, soaping and washing each other. Ordinary conversation and everyday activities become eroticized. The perpetrator tests to see if the child will keep secrets and whether she will reciprocate by fondling back. The abuse is maintained by a mixture of rewards and punishment. The child is trapped by the responsibility that is being put on him or her. *Degrading the victim* and making it the child's fault completes the grooming process.

EFFECTS OF SEXUAL ABUSE

Sexually abused children feel betrayed and respond to being used as a sexual object. They feel spoilt, debased and violated. Bewildering feelings of guilt are mixed with anger and shame. It is not surprising such children have a poor self-image. Sometimes these feelings are taken out on the community by delinquent acts and sometimes on themselves by self-destructive behaviour, eating disturbances, depression and suicides (Fromuth 1986, Harrison et al 1984, Oates 1990, Tong et al 1987). De Young (1982) discovered that 79 per cent of the incest victims studied had predominantly hostile feelings towards their mothers who they felt had not protected them, while 52 per cent were hostile towards the abuser. Research has also discovered that victims later in adulthood can have an aversion to sexual activity, or can become promiscuous or involved in prostitution (James and Meyerding 1977). The rage inside can 'erupt as a pattern of abuse against offspring in the next generation' (Summit 1983).

Male victims
John Sebold in 1987 gathered together 22 therapists who had treated male victims and they drew up a list of nine indicators. The most dramatic is the presence of *homophobic concerns*. These often come out most in physical altercations that revolve around issues of the sexually abused boys' sexual preferences. The adolescents were anxious not to be thought gay and played up to females. They would put down others who they thought had homosexual inclinations. The second characteristic was the use of *threatening behaviour* to assure themselves that they could ward off future sexual approaches. Sadly the boys' ability to intimidate and overpower may lead to a temporary sense of power and aggression but it is followed by depression and a need for another dose of aggression. The aggressive cycle is thus initiated.

Infantile behaviour, preoccupation with sexual thoughts and with younger males *masturbation* in public were all significant features. The researchers said they were particularly irritated by the way that ordinary routine *language was sexualized* and sniggered about.

Initially the boys tended to show little concern with their appearance but after the sexually abusive event the victims can become *compulsive* about their presentation. Younger children suffer from *eneuresis* and *encropresis* while the researchers also noted numerous physical complaints. The awful feelings of helplessness were expressed by suicide attempts.

The most interesting indication mentioned by nearly all the therapists was *fire-setting behaviour*. Also, though not mentioned by this project, Justice and Justice (1979) noted male prostitution as an indicator of earlier sexual abuse.

Back to the slippery slope

To return to the slippery slope: the next signpost is *misogynous* incest. This would involve perpetrators who are in conflict with their own mothers. They are violent and punishing towards all women. The child is regarded as a possession, as is his wife. Control and power is at its zenith! Power is the theme and often is a way of compensating for the mediocre life a man leads outside his home.

We now come to the group most often blamed for sexual abuse – *paedophiles*. Very roughly it is possible to divide this group up and look firstly at the fixated paedophile. His unresolved problems mean he is permanently arrested in his psycho-social maturation. He is attracted primarily and exclusively to children and young people. He feels comfortable and satisfied with such activity and experiences no intense feelings of guilt, shame or remorse until afterwards. He experiences his orientation as a compulsion which he says he cannot resist. Adults do not turn him on. He is unlikely to change and therefore is a constant risk to children. The second group (although Glaser and Frosh (1988) doubt this group exists) are men who originally preferred adults for sexual gratification but when adult relationships become conflictual the original choice is replaced by the child. Such a man says he feels guilt, shame and disgust, embarrassment and remorse but this comes after the abuse. During the event he has partial disassociation and doesn't think about what he is doing suspending his usual values.

Slipping further down the slope we are looking at *pressurized sexual contact* and *forced contact*. In the first group the perpetrator uses enticement, indoctrination, persuasion and cajolement. 'We've had fun at the zoo, now you do this in return.' He does not use force. At some level he cares, but the emotional cost is severe. Sex is in the service of need for physical contact. The words used by the perpetrator are that the child is innocent, loving, open and affectionate. In the second group sex-force offenders use threats and intimidation. They exploit the child's naivety and hopelessness.

Still sliding down we are looking at *exploitive and sadistic assault*. In the former circumstances the child is the object of sexual relief. The child is an outlet solely for sexual gratification – a disposable object to be used then discarded. The words used by the perpetrator to describe the child are weak, defenceless, helpless, unable to resist and easily controlled. He may not intend to do harm but his lack of concern for the consequences and the emotional cost to the child is totally destructive.

In the next small group are sadistic assaulters. This group derives pleasure from hurting the child. Sexuality and aggression become one. The child is the target of rage and cruelty. The child has to be degraded in order to get excitement and gratification. The child has to be choked, tortured, hurt and punished. The perpetrators plan the sexual abuse a long time in advance. It's all about domination and anger. Everything he hates about himself is represented by the child, so the child has to suffer. The use of 'rent boys' may come into this group. Torment and suffering are part of the sexual gratification. Sexuality and power are in the service of anger.

In the deep mud at the bottom of the slope it is not easy to tease out different categories. They tend to merge into each other. *The child rapist* really confuses masculinity with power. He needs to punish. He is attracted to violence. He is dangerous because his perverse feelings of guilt are mixed with his fear of discovery. Because of this mixture he is likely to kill the child.

At the very bottom is *ritualistic* abuse. These perpetrators set up rituals to fulfil a variety of forbidden fantasies. They try to solve their conflicts through sexual activities which go beyond the limits of any socially accepted sexual practices – to explore what is most forbidden. So animals are killed in front of the children, masks and costumes are worn. Drinking of blood and urine, magical surgery, digging up of graves and devil worship all play a part. The use of religious objects is all part of the process.

Finkelhor (Finkelhor et al 1988) defines ritualistic abuse as that which 'occurs in a context linked to some symbols or group acitivity that have a religious, magical or supernatural connotation and where invocation of these symbols or activities repeated over time, is used to frighten and intimidate children.'

As so much has been sensationalized it is useful to divide ritualistic abuse into three:

Cults
The hallmark of this type of ritualistic abuse is the existence of an elaborated belief system and the attempt to create a particular spiritual or social system through practices that involve physical, sexual and emotional abuse (Finkelhor et al 1988). The sexual abuse of children is not the ultimate goal but a method of inducing a religious or mystical experience or the loss of ego boundaries. For the adult involved, it is an attempt to keep the group together, to corrupt a new generation and induct new members into evil practices.

Pseudo-ritualistic abuse
This is where ritualistic practices are used to stop the children from telling about the sexual abuse: to intimidate the victims and to discredit their testimony, because no one will believe the child's story. How right they are!

Psycho-pathological ritualism
This is when the sexual abuse and rituals are part of the perpetrator's obsessive and delusional system. This may involve sexual preoccupations or sexual compulsions. For instance the abuser may develop an obsession around the child's genitals, believing they are evil and have to be cleansed and purified.

Possible therapeutic approaches are outlined in the next section. The protection of the children involved must always be our first priority. However this becomes even more significant when we realize that our chances of effectively working with perpetrators at the bottom of the slope are very slender indeed.

WORKING WITH FAMILIES WHERE SEXUAL ABUSE HAS TAKEN PLACE

No one person can help the sexually abusing family. It is an interdisciplinary task. The work starts for the whole team as soon as the sexual abuse has been discovered with the joint investigation by social services and the police. Interdisciplinary work is no easy matter as bureaucracy and feelings get in the way. For instance, social workers may be so incensed with the perpetrator they conveniently 'forget' him, especially if he is in prison or has left the home, and consequently just work with mother and child. The probation officer say, entrapped by the time it takes to get the case heard and not wanting to feel the pain of what the client has done to a child, leaves co-operation till late on in the process, when perhaps release is considered or an order made.

Interdisciplinary team
The first task is to consider who does what and when and to decide who should be in the team. What is the task of the probation officer? What is the role of the social worker? How is the nursery nurse to fit into the team? What is the programme for the residential worker? When does the investigatory social worker hand over to the long-term team? How can the women's group support the mother and coordinate with work done in the group for mothers of sexually abused children? The tasks delegated to the school need to be thoroughly discussed and interrelated into the whole programme. The scenario may be anything from the abuser being in prison to the child being allowed to remain at home with the family unit intact.

Before any work with the family begins, all those who are to make a professional contribution need to engage in self-work and accept all information has to be shared. There can be no more secrets, either in the family or amongst professionals.

Self-work
Whatever our status or sex we may have had a range of

satisfactions or dissatisfactions from our own sexual encounters, whether they are with the opposite or same sex. Some of us may have been sexually abused ourselves and some of us may even be sexually attracted to children. All this must be honestly faced.

Unless we work with our conflicts, confusions, disgusts and deep satisfactions they will skew our work. Nothing makes us so aware of our own sexuality and anger, as sexual abuse. Male workers may be seen as people who have the potential to perpetrate sexual acts. Female workers can be seen by victims as representing the mother who they feel didn't protect them.

Just because we are trained professional people it does not mean we are free of punitive attitudes. We may have worked with ourselves once but we may still have to repeat it every time we read the evidence. It sometimes helps to remember that often sexually abusing parents were themselves reared by uncaring parents. Without help they court rejection from partners, friends and acquaintances. They stew in a state of chronic resentment which they discharge through hostile acts unconsciously intended to be self-punishing.

This work is not for anyone who wants to play the role of 'Mr/Ms Nice Guy'. The more effective you are the less you will be liked by some of the clients. It is essential to see through the 'flight into health' as perpetrators try to con you into believing they are cured. Equally we have to watch in ourselves and those attending the child protection conference the assumptions that 'all men are' . . . / 'all women are' . . . and challenge inside ourselves the concept of conquest sex. Bearing all this in mind it might be useful to have a systematic, planned approach.

FOUR-POINT PLAN (Meinig and Bonner 1990)

This model looks a lot of work. It is, although some of the programme will be going on at the same time and some of the tasks may only involve a couple of sessions.

I Individual work is required with
   (a) the mother
   (b) the child
   (c) the perpetrator

(d) the siblings and significant others.

The individual work will give the team an indication of whether the perpetrator can be sufficiently changed to be allowed home, whether the mother can protect her child or has to face the horrendous decision of choosing between the child and her partner.

II If the initial assessment leads to a decision to work towards family reunion and this is also what the victim wants, work is then done with
   (a) mother and victim
   (b) perpetrator and victim.
III Then follows marital and family counselling.
IV Then time is spent looking for situations where all parties can continue to get support.

Let us now flesh out the plan.

Ia Work with the mother (Bentovim 1988, Erooga and Masson 1989, Sgroi 1982)

Aims
In no way should it be suggested that the mother is to blame; she is the lynchpin of any work and must be empowered. The aim, whether it be individual work or in a group, will be to help her to accept and believe her child. She must acknowledge that the children have been affected by the victimization and that the act of molestation by the offender was purposeful. It may take time for her to come to terms with her partner's original denials and the temptation will be to minimize his behaviour. As work progresses she may have to learn to recognize the tell-tale signs that he is slipping back into his old abusive ways. The important thing is that this time she will seek help and institute protective measures. Perhaps one of her hardest tasks is to lessen her emotional and even financial dependence on the offender.

The non-offending parent may need practical help with prison visiting and coping on a lower income. She may be chronically depressed and need medical and social help. Above all, group or individual help must provide the space to allow her to feel through whether she wants to keep her partner or her child, if that choice has to be made for the protection of the child. If she is rushed into choosing her child, there is a danger that when everything has settled down, the very thing that attracted her to her partner in the first place will encourage the couple secretly to get back together again and sexual abuse will re-occur. This time the child will not disclose.

As well as the group run by the social worker, mothers may need the additional support of a women's group, especially if they have been abused themselves. In the social worker's group the mothers need to discuss their wide range of feelings. To start with they may need to deny that anything has happened at all. They are angry with the child, feel let down and isolated. Feelings of having failed as a wife and mother can be overwhelming and the mothers may need a lot of nurturing and support. Their self-image has taken a bashing. Assertion training can be very valuable.

The opening sessions of the therapeutic group by the social worker will allow for ventilation of feelings: exploration of what it means to be 'piggy in the middle'. Not until time has been spent looking at the confusion of her feelings can the mother look at her role and understand what happened.

The group will then tend to go through a phase when the mothers feel 'all men are bastards' and have unreasonable expectations of partners and children. This is the time when setting limits on their children's behaviour has to be discussed, as their guilt makes them swing between being over-indulgent and over-strict with them.

Anger then usually returns as the major issue. The mother too has been made a victim. This is true but she has to realize that she chose her partner, the children did not. Art and role-plays are often useful methods of getting the anger out and helping the mothers gain a personal identity of being a woman first, then a wife and mother.

A lot of work needs to be focused on the methods of communication within the family and outside it. The group is a useful setting for social-skills training and learning how to build up networks and use support systems. The support of other mothers in the same boat helps them all to face the task of re-defining self and having to learn new coping skills.

Ib Work with the child (MacFarlane et al 1986)
The feeling that one is unique, isolated, and the only person in the world who has been abused is best challenged by being in a

group, but work with sexually abused children should not be delayed because there are no groups in the area.

Obviously the style and approach of the group must be fashioned to meet the age and needs of the members. However at least six target areas have to be tackled.

Damaged goods syndrome
Children who have been sexually abused often suffer from what Sgroi (1982) called the damaged goods syndrome. If the abuse has been painful children often fear they may be damaged internally. A sensitive medical may be required to reassure the child or to spell out honestly what needs to be put right. Moreover sexually abused children are often treated differently and it is a strange phenomenon that they are regarded as 'fair game' for further abuse. This has to be confronted.

Self-esteem work
Abused children need to be able to feel good about their bodies and to develop self-esteem. With younger children, drawing self-portraits and creating the trophy they would most like to win and presenting it to the self can be useful building exercises. Corder (Corder et al 1990) creates a story in which a child is abused, works through it and comes out stronger in the end. Each child has a series of faces, perhaps drawn on cardboard plates, representing a range of feelings: guilt, anger, fear and depression. As the narrator stops at salient points the children show how they think the child in the story felt by holding up their 'feeling' plates. At the conclusion there are a range of chants shouted as loudly as possible:

> 'I'm a good person, I'm proud of me.
> I've been through a lot, look how strong I've got.'

> 'That was then, but this is now.
> I won't be abused and I know how.'

The story can thus release and help the children talk about their own personal experiences and feelings. Above all the children need to believe nothing was their fault. Nothing, but nothing, a child does, justifies the sexual approaches of an adult.

Learning how to be affectionate

As has already been said, the effect of sexual abuse is that the victim does not know the difference between affectionate and sexualized behaviour. Children need to be re-taught what is good and what is bad touch, how they can protect themselves and that they have a right to say no. Sharing a terminology for sexual parts of the body can help a child learn the words to be used to tell if there is further abuse.

Fears

Sexually abused children can still feel frightened at night even if the perpetrator is locked up in prison. Frightening dreams can interrupt sleep. Ways have to be found to make them feel safe. One child I helped by persuading the parents to allow the dog to sleep on the bed and act as guardian.

Sex education

Sensitivity has to be used here, as people in some cultures are not happy about their daughters being taught the facts of life, even after being sexually abused. However, straightforward information about bodily functions can be reassuring and facilitate the ability to see sex as a proper part of loving and part of a co-equal relationship.

Feelings towards the perpetrator

Time must be set aside in the group for the children to share their role confusion and mixed feelings towards the abuser, and the effects of broken trust and loss of a parent. The child has to learn how to be a child again, a person in his or her own right, separate, and not an object to be used by another. There can be no more secrets in the family and as part of the four-point plan the child too has to learn some of the tell-tale signs of the father starting to slip back into his old ways. This helps the child to protect his or herself, knowing that the mother will protect and also seek outside help.

Ic Work with the perpetrator

A useful way of beginning is to consider Finkelhor's four hurdles (Finkelhor 1984). To become a sexual abuser a person has to have a motive to abuse. Then that person has to find ways of overcoming his internal inhibitors which prevent him from acting out his wishes. Next he has to overcome his external inhibitors. Lastly he has to overcome the child's resistance.

Perpetrators are subtly very powerful. Remembering the time and skill he took to create the victim in the family or outside it, it is worth bearing in mind that he can make workers into victims too (Moore 1990). It is a particularly difficult area of work as so often the abuser was himself a victim. The worker may get lost between the past and the present. If this happens the worker becomes impotent.

A sex-abuser can seduce us by his helplessness. He plays the game – 'How could you do this to me?' 'What you accuse me of is out of character' – and attempts to blind us by recounting his good works. At the time of disclosure by the child, he minimizes the offence by suggesting it was just a one-off occasion. He was drunk at the time and didn't know which was his wife and which was the child! 'You misunderstand what was seen.' 'I'd just had a bath.' 'I was just comforting her'.

The abuser may use political arguments. 'If we lived in X or Y country it would be OK, so why make such a big deal about it?' He may blame the victim or hook us by saying that treatment has just begun so why disrupt it all by reporting this tiny slip. A final defence may be 'I'm saved, so God wouldn't allow me to do it, so I don't need any social work help.'

In order not to become a victim, workers have to have the ability to maintain a professional stance and not be blown off course by all the pain, anger, fear and guilt that is around. Workers have to resist the temptation to rescue the client from his pain. The abuser can swing through a whole range of feelings in an unnerving way. He starts by showing great self-hatred; he then acts seductively towards the worker, playing the child to the worker's parent; then he is over-compliant and swings into despair, anger and even violence (Horton et al 1990, O'Connell et al 1990).

Workers must be very realistic. Sex offenders can fool the worker, and themselves, that progress has been made. A useful maxim is that sex offenders cannot be cured but a large number can learn to control their behaviour. Progress must be seen in small steps and can only be achieved if worker and client are truly committed.

Lastly, work with the perpetrator has to be confrontational (Cowburn 1990, Wyre 1989). Sex offenders are secretive and resist revealing or changing behaviour. They cover up, defend and rationalize. All the workers in the team have to challenge the perpetrator's cognitive thinking that allows him to continue offending. Distortions such as 'The child was not harmed, she really liked it' must be confronted. All the workers in the team need always to describe what happened in explicit ways, between themselves, and with the client, without embarrassment. So it is not 'You abused your child' but 'You put your fingers into your child's vagina.'

Denial
Child protection conferences need to know, before considering return of the child, what specific progress has been made with the abuser. Vague phrases like 'He has made progress' are dangerous. Salter (1988) has produced an excellent model upon which to test what progress the client has truly made. At one time we believed that sex offenders either denied everything or admitted everything. We now realize things are far more complicated. According to Salter perpetrators are like icebergs: 'They only expose a fraction of the problem. Disarmingly they make idiosyncratic distinctions in degrees of blame, often unintelligible to an outsider and tailor their stories accordingly.' We must never assume the abuser has no reason to lie, nor that his version of the story is necessarily the correct one. Salter has created a spectrum with six segments; the nearer the client is to the first segment the more the risk to the child.

First segment This client has an alibi for the day. Even if the evidence is very strong he and his family cling on to their story. He doesn't accept responsibility because the event did not occur. He does not admit planning the abuse and responds with righteous indignation. It's easy to be fooled into thinking *he* is the victim of the system. He is very believable.

Second segment Rather than 'I was not there' it is 'I'm not that sort of person'. He does not admit harming the child and has little shame or guilt. He has no reason to change because he did not do it.

Third segment This group of abusers admit to part of the behaviour but deny the rest. They will profess a desire for treatment but withhold key information. They usually refuse to admit to sexual fantasies or planning and equivocate as to how responsible they are for the offence. Minimizing the harm to the child is the order of the day. They have no sense of internalized guilt and they underestimate the difficulty of change. Just deciding not to abuse is enough, they feel.

Fourth segment This group admit to the extent of their behaviour but minimize the seriousness. The victim will be quick to recover. By denying the seriousness of his behaviour the perpetrator can protect himself from his guilt. All his cognitive distortions give him permission to go on. He presses to return home but then refuses to co-operate with any treatment programme.

Fifth segment This character admits his behaviour, 'accepts its seriousness but denies responsibility'. He blames alcohol, his wife or his stress at work.

Sixth segment You're in with a chance with this group! He doesn't deny his offence and admits the full extent of his sexual deviance. He tells the same story as the victim. He will share the way he planned and groomed the victim. The vital thing is, he doesn't see change as easy. Often he gives himself a bad press by recognizing his temptation to backslide and is nervous about family reunification. Above all he recognizes he can't undo the harm he has done.

Three-pronged approach
Work with sex offenders often has to be three-pronged. *Case work by itself can just lead to a more insightful but continuing sex offender.* To quote Salter again, 'Family therapy addresses the non-sexual problems that offenders so often flee from by sexually acting out. Group therapy addresses particular cognitive distortions ... Behaviour therapy decreases deviant arousal patterns and gives offenders tools for self control.'

A battery of programmes needs to be worked out together with the social work approach.

(a) *Responsibility work* gets the client to take full responsibility for what he has done, moving from passivity to responsibility.

(b) *Constant challenge to the cognitive distortions* 'It just happened,' is not acceptable.
(c) *Life maps and sex maps* enable the client to come to terms with what happened to them in the past.
(d) *Working out their cycle of offending* and learning the point where it is possible to break the cycle (Ryan 1987).
(e) *Anger* control.
(f) *Depression* control.
(g) Practical ways of *controlling urges*.
(h) Building up *self-esteem*.
(i) *Social skills training*.
(j) *Sex education*.
(k) *Victim awareness* helps them to acknowledge the damage they have done and to learn that children are people with feelings.
(l) *Ways to stop playing the role of victims themselves* Whatever happened to them they must not themselves abuse children.

Id   Work with the siblings and significant others

At least one session must be given to the other children. Split loyalties have to be addressed. They may be jealous of the attention the abused child was given originally and is now getting. They may be angry with the child for breaking up the family. Perhaps they are guilty at not noticing what was going on and therefore not preventing the abuse. New opportunities may have to be created to get communication going again and make sense of what happened.

Work may have to be undertaken with say a paternal grandparent who is constantly undermining the mother by saying her son could never have done such an awful thing as sexually abuse his child.

IIa   Work with mother/child victim

Mother and child have to face together the child's feelings of anger and bewilderment. They now need to build up a strong protective alliance between the two of them: to re-create an emotional closeness which has been destroyed by what has happened.

IIb   Work with perpetrator and victim

As part of the total programme there must be at least one

carefully planned session when child and perpetrator meet, for the offender to take responsibility for what happened. This can then release the child's feelings. It then becomes possible to look at the ambivalence about events. It will enable the victim to separate love for the perpetrator from hatred of his behaviour.

III Marital and family counselling

The precise sequence of work can only be left to the skill of the interdisciplinary team. However after work with the dyads of mother and child and perpetrator and child, then marital and family counselling can begin.

Marital work

A couple who can give each other nurture are less likely to turn to the child for comfort. A couples group can therefore be most valuable. Belonging to such a group defines the couple as adults separate from their children, a boundary that needs to be reinforced in sexually abusing families. But whether there is a group or joint sessions, the areas most useful to look at are the abuse itself and then the marital conflicts. The couple often need help in communicating. As one perpetrator said, 'This is the first time in our marriage that we have ever been able to communicate.' The worker's task is to facilitate the couple to tell each other what they find sexually and emotionally satisfying. Power and how it is shared needs to be discussed and different patterns of responses considered. The management of the children is often a tense area because as a result of the help given, the mother has become empowered and is playing a stronger, more protective role.

Family work

There must be some sessions with the whole family and these are more useful in the final phase of treatment. Three areas have proved valuable to discuss: communication patterns, rules and knowledge about sex, and family systems. Having a whole family together is a useful way of challenging pathological communication patterns. This is the time when the worker can help the family to expose family secrets and open up communication between family members. Each family member can be asked to talk about what happened and to express their feelings about what they are hearing. This is when it is helpful for the perpetrator publicly to take responsibility for his abuse. The discussion should then lead on to what will happen if the perpetrator should ever attempt to repeat the abuse. It should be clear within the family who will be told and what the consequences will be. Having opened up communication channels other key issues should be discussed as a total family.

The second area of work is to do 'with sexuality and practices that may increase the risk of sexual stimulation and sexual abuse' (Faller 1988). So often sexuality is not discussed within sexually abusing families. It therefore becomes a taboo subject holding 'much fascination'. This also means the children have no way of differentiating sex from other interactions and do not recognize inappropriate sexual activity. Information shared by the whole family group with the worker can thus become a common body of knowledge about appropriate and inappropriate behaviour.

During this discussion the worker can discover family practices that exacerbate the risk of sexual stimulation and abuse. The task of the worker will be to spell out why these practices are inappropriate and to help the family draw up a set of new rules. However the rules must be feasible otherwise they will become a source of resentment and will not be followed.

The last area to be addressed is *family systems*. Unless the interdisciplinary team can help the family to change these patterns the chances of sexual abuse recurring are extremely high. If it were possible to take a photograph the family systems (over-simplified to aid description) would fall roughly into the following five patterns.

1   In the first model the father is the dominant one. The family present to the world an idealized picture. A dicey marriage is denied. The child moves towards father and becomes afraid of the relationship. She tells mother. Mother's response is, 'How could you say such an awful thing

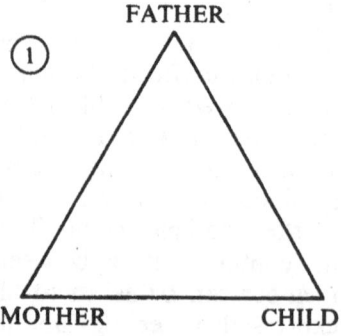

about your dear father?' Unable to get support, the child moves closer and closer to father and sexual abuse takes place.

2 Mother in this pattern is the dominant person. She treats father and child as a couple of adolescents. Gradually the roles become abusive.

3 Here, almost as a paradox, the child is the powerful one. She/he sacrifices herself/himself and allows herself/himself to be abused in order to keep mum and dad together. Keeping her/his parents together is the paramount aim and under no circumstances does she/he want to tell the authorities.

4 In this pattern father and child pair and push mother out of the relationship. The relationship becomes abusive and mother finds it hard if not impossible to regain her appropriate role.

5 The last defies visual description. This is the situation where parents and children are in a confused, conflicting way, locked in abusing relationships. Dad is abusing the girls and the boys. Mother may also be abusing the children.

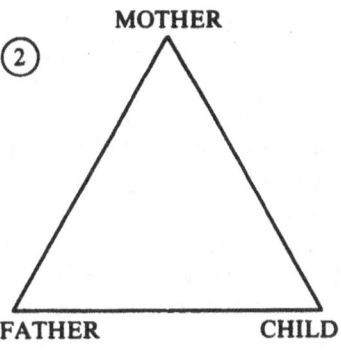

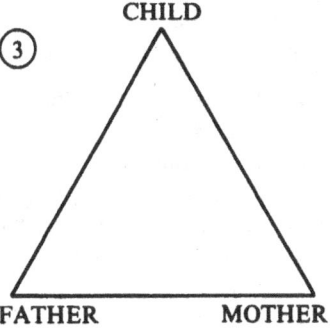

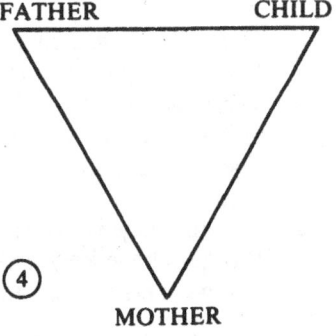

IV Continuing support

If the family has been split, the reunification has to take place in gradual stages. It can begin by meetings in public neutral places, then day visits to the home. Finally overnight stays can be gradually extended. Each stage has to be monitored by the appropriate professionals. The time will then come when the case is terminated.

However, as sex-offending is an addiction and is never cured, it is of inestimable value if there can be a named agency or individual who could be contacted in periods of stress. This would be a form of prevention.

Final comment

As a postscript, using the work of Fawcett (1987) I have drawn up a list of areas the interdisciplinary team need to be assured about before children are allowed to return home and the family reunited. The order is not significant.

- The perpetrator has now taken full responsibility for the offence.
- The generational boundaries are now restored.
- No one is now special in the family.
- No one blames the victimized child.
- There is now clear and open communication within the family.
- There is now a good relationship between victim and mother and the mother will protect and seek professional help if necessary.
- The family have improved their problem-solving processes.
- There is a child-protection plan that all are committed to making work.
- The offender has changed and has realistic coping mechanisms to cope with his impulses.
- Everyone including the children can spot if the perpetrator's behaviour is similar to that before the offence.
- The workers know how not to become victims of the clients.
- The marriage is now a nurturing one.
- Workers have knowledge of working with sex offenders.
- The workers are sensitively and systematically supervised.

If within the scenario the perpetrator is either locked away in prison with no work done with him before he returns to the family, or has been banned from one family only to move into another, leaving the first family angry and confused, the trust of all the children involved is betrayed. Disclosure should be just the beginning of work not the end, and unless work is done with all those involved the child will remain vulnerable.

WOMEN CAN ... AND DO*

Women can and do sexually abuse children. In making this statement I do not want to divert attention from the fact that the vast majority of sexual offenders are male; nor to remove gender issues from the discussion; nor to dilute the women's movement's contribution to the understanding of sexual abuse, as an abuse of power. In fact, as we look at women abusers this argument takes on a new and significant meaning. In at least one study all the women abusers had been sexually abused by men when young (Mathews et al 1989).

Early researchers did not look at female offenders and unconsciously we have stopped recognizing the possibility; consequently children are not protected. Mathis (1972) dismissed female abusers as so rare as to be of little significance. 'Women are viewed as sexually harmless to children.' Unfortunately these ideas are not dead. A worker recently had the experience of actually seeing a woman orally masturbating her child. When she recounted this observation to her team she was told she was imagining it. Interpretations were made about her own psychological state as she was pregnant at the time. It was not until another worker who was not enmeshed in the system allowed her to talk out what had happened that she gave validity to what she had seen. As Sgroi (1975) said, 'Recognition of sexual molestation in a child is dependent upon the individual's inherent willingness to entertain the possibility that the condition may exist.'

According to Faller (1987) the top four abusive acts by women are group sex, fondling, oral and digital sex. Often we are only dealing with reported cases. Women 'are generally regarded as being out of place in the criminal justice system', a factor that helps them 'negotiate the various escape routes within it'. Women offenders are thus less likely to come to public attention (Allen 1990).

---

* This section (pp 73–76) appeared as an article in *Community Care*, March 1991, and is reproduced with the Editor's permission.

In 1969 De Francis found three per cent of perpetrators were women. The National Incidence Study whose figures were reanalysed by Finkelhor and Russell (Finkelhor 1984) found 13 per cent in the case of female victims and 24 per cent in the case of male victims were females.

The American Humane Association suggests 14 per cent of offences against boys and six per cent against girls are committed by women. But criticism can be made of these figures, as it is not possible to distinguish clearly between women perpetrators who committed the abuse and those who allowed it to happen.

Groth and Russell (1984) found just over half of a sample of sex offenders had been victimized when they were young, and of these 25 per cent had been victimized by a female. The same figure of 51 per cent of a sample of attenders at a Parents United Conference had been victimized and 33 per cent had been victimized by females.

It is difficult and perhaps a little dangerous to try to compile a composite picture from the paucity of research material. There is no agreement as to what is sexual abuse. Researchers are looking at different types of offences.

In Mathews et al (1989) many of the women offenders had been charged with other forms of child abuse and only revealed sexually abusing their children when they felt completely safe with their therapist and were therefore less likely to find their way into official statistics.

It is this study which perhaps provides the clearest categorization. The authors, approaching the subject from a feminist perspective, divided their clients into three groups: the *teacher/lover*, the *predisposed* and the *male coerced*.

The teacher/lover group tend to be defensive and generally minimize the negative impact of their behaviour. They may be angry and act out their anger. Mathews et al (1989) quote the case of Ann. Her family was chaotic, she felt lonely and alienated from her family. Because of her deformity she played with younger children who were not as cruel as her age mates. She felt more powerful with the younger children. At 14 she was sexually abused by a gang of boys.

After a destructive adolescence she became a prostitute and slept rough. After a failed marriage she made a liaison that was more violent than all her other relationships. She had two boys and was helped to parent them by the mother of her boyfriend.

She managed to break away from the relationship and decided never to trust men again. She met Elliot a needy boy who was in residential care and had no relationships with his own mother. When she was 40 and he 14 they became sexually involved. However when challenged by a friend, Elliott was overheard by Ann to say 'I wouldn't fuck that old cow.' She tried to get reassurance from Elliot but decided he, too, was using her. This relationship did not come to light until she was in treatment for playing sexual games with three children of the neighbourhood.

In the predisposed group were women who mainly sexually abused their own children. Often they are from families where sexual abuse has been going on for years. Bonnie, in Mathews' study, was fondled by the age of four, and introduced to intercourse and oral sex by six. Because of her early abuse she was not able to relate to peers.

Women of this group do not enjoy sex, feel impotent and cannot say 'no'. They find solace in drugs, alcohol and overeating. Because they are hungry for love they make dangerous relationships. They may physically abuse their own children saying they want to hurt as they were hurt. They have low self-esteem, distorted thinking and feelings of persecution. Bonnie felt her mother hated her. Her father and grandfather had both sexually abused her. She tried to get out of the trap by attempting suicide. Her adult life was just as traumatic and she decided not to relate to men. Bonnie verbally, physically and sexually abused her daughter 'just needing to feel close to someone physically'.

The third group, the male coerced, feels powerless, passive and dependent on men. Kris yearned for someone to take care of her and felt a bad marriage was better than no marriage at all. She came from an uncaring family, was abused by a stranger, taunted by the children at school and kept people at a safe psychological distance.

She was pressurized into marriage by her parents. The first year was good. However, her husband gradually become more and more violent towards her and the children. Then he began to beat and sexually abuse them. She tried to escape by taking sleeping pills and drinking.

Next her husband introduced the sex game of 'spin the bottle' and invited adult friends to join in. Later Kris played the game with the children alone. 'Having sex with my sons was more enjoyable than having sex with my husband, because I have some control.'

This group overlaps with one of the five categories drawn up by Faller, who uses the title polyincestuous. It is also the largest group.

Women do sexually abuse. In 1987 Freeman-Longo noted that 40 per cent of rapists in his study had been sexually abused by females and 'none of them had reported it to be a pleasant experience'. To ignore the possibility of women abusers means some children are left unprotected and the devastating exploitation of power in all its forms ricochets down the generations.

Working with women perpetrators

Women are different from men. This is nowhere more apparent than when looking at sex offences. According to Mathews (Mathews et al 1989) critical confrontation does not work. Female sex-offenders know their behaviour is wrong and rarely blame their victims. Unfortunately as so few women offenders reach court, they tend to be lumped in with male offenders and treated in the same way. The exceptions are the work of Mathews et al (1989), Barnett et al (1989) and Scavo (1989).

Mathews lays great stress on the importance of the style of the worker, whether group or individual skills are used. Because the woman offender is so emotionally fused with her offence the worker's style has to challenge the behaviour but not the person. The aim is to help the woman separate herself from her behaviour, to take responsibility and develop empathy, rather than respond with a sense of shame and loathing. So according to Mathews the style of the worker has to be non-judgemental, understanding and accepting: not badgering the client. A group must become a safe place to discuss the abusive behaviour and to gain the feeling of not being alone. Healing seems to begin when the group helps the female client feel less needy and more able to tackle the areas they need to work on themselves.

They are often slow starters. After all they are people who could not trust anyone in their lives. Their past experiences give them little hope things will change in the future, so they find it difficult to share feelings, hopes and opinions. If they are part of a group they begin to trust individuals and then very slowly expand their trust to involve others. Because of their low self-esteem they lack social skills. After all, sharing of feelings has always seemed to them like weakness. It reminds them of their own early experiences when their emotional vulnerability was taken advantage of and they now feel it will happen all over again.

Help can perhaps be divided into three stages: looking at what led up to the offence and what patterns of behaviour need to change; then looking at what lessons have to be learned and cognitive distortions challenged; lastly, areas that need to be worked upon.

What leads up to the behaviour
In the Mathews study all the women had previously been abused. In the Barnett group only two out of the six women said they had been abused (Barnett et al 1989). However the authors felt their information was incomplete. To those who have not been abused it doesn't seem so significant, but it is a real move forward when the women can make a connection between their own abuse and what they did to the children. They had never realized they did not deserve to be abused. Women offenders tend to blame themselves for their original victimization. They believe themselves to be evil and to have done something to bring their own abuse on to themselves. The delicate task for the worker is to challenge their attitude towards their own abuse without allowing it to become an excuse for the abuse of their victims.

Barnett et al (1989) found that helping their women clients to examine alternative strategies of behaviour instead of the committing of their offences was helpful. Often this brings up the whole issue of dependence upon drugs and alcohol. It was painful for them to see they could have refused to collude with their co-offenders and instead leave the situation or remove the children from the scene, seeking support from someone else. Addressing these issues brings up feelings of powerlessness and inadequacy. These feelings can then be discussed. As one client said, 'I feel I could and should have stopped what took place ... It was my place to do so' (Mathews 1989).

Depending upon a male, feelings of neediness and isolation are three themes that are often significant in the lead up to the women sexually abusing their children, or colluding with the dominating male partner. 'There has to be a male in my life otherwise I would think I was a nobody.' 'I'm good for nothing' (Mathews et al 1989).

Individual or group work has to be targetted to build up self-esteem and challenge feelings of worthlessness. The women can then become whole people capable of caring for themselves and can be happy. One mother described the process as like a flower 'starting to blossom', reaching for the sun. If patterns of behaviour are to change, the group or the worker has to be committed and believe the client *can* change. It does need courage and strength. Group members have to learn how to confront each other in a positive, honest and caring way, recognizing the danger signals that will lead to negative behaviour in themselves and the children becoming victims.

Lessons to be learned

When we come to the second and third aspects, much of the approach overlaps with work with male offenders. The women need to learn what is positive and negative touch, to know the boundaries. Sex between an adult and a child is wrong. Adults can say no to sex. Children never deserve to be sexually abused. Often the mothers have to learn what is sexually abusive and how children can be damaged by witnessing sexual behaviour.

Like male offenders they have to learn that children are human beings, with the worker making sure the child victim is seen as a real person in all the discussions that may take place. Many mothers who have sexually abused their children have to discuss with their worker whether they are aiming to be reunited with their children or whether it is in the best interests of the children to be adopted. If the aim is the former some time has to be spent on developing good parenting skills.

Areas to be worked on

Lastly in a group or in individual work, the woman offender like her male counterpart has to take full responsibility for her actions. They have abused their power. They need to learn how to express their anger: to be able to be angry without being destructive. They must learn that their dependence upon alcohol and drugs is all part of the same self-destructive feelings of worthlessness. They can be their own persons. Assertion training may help them learn they do not have to fulfil the needs of others or be pushed around.

Families

A final point about families. Some female abusers may be adolescents. The family must therefore be involved in the treatment process. The family will often try to minimize the offence and become overly protective of the client, blaming the victim or the victim's family. Sometimes the family swings the other way, rejecting the adolescent and assuming a hopeless attitude towards the helping process. It is often at the stage of discovery of the adolescent's offence that the earlier perpetrator's abuse is revealed. It is important if possible for the original abuser to be identified, confronted and reported to the police.

Adult women offenders may need to go back to their original families and challenge some of the original family myths. Often their sexual victimization had been kept secret from the family. Sometimes they were seen as privileged when in fact they were abused. Siblings were often unaware why the abuser originally had difficulty in school and could not make friends. The family secret must be exploded, to release the client, so that progress can be made.

If we can discard gender-biased stereotypes we may be able to recognize the women abuser. Having recognized the phenomenon we may be able to work with the woman abuser. Remembering what Sgroi (1975) said (quoted on p 73), recognition may lead to many more offenders being discovered or referring themselves for help. This is crucial for the children involved. To be sexually abused by your mother is a double betrayal, a double abuse.

5 Neglect of Neglect – Child Neglect

Imagine the following scenario. It is a cold Monday morning, you are a social services duty officer. The phone rings; it is a sexual abuse referral. Your adrenalin starts to rise, so does your anxiety. A buzz runs round the whole office. The phone rings again but this time it is a neglect referral. Everyone has difficulty in smothering a faint yawn.

WHY WE NEGLECT NEGLECT

We neglect neglect. There are a number of complex interacting reasons. To begin with neglect is estimated to be five times more prevalent than physical abuse (Wolock and Horowitz 1984, Young 1981). Neglect cases are therefore more common and never likely to be popular. The dynamics within the neglecting family often lead to a situation that drains workers. To tackle neglect properly confronts politicians with huge resource implications. So corporately we deny and rationalize. In fact neglect cases are less often registered.

Human beings are strange animals. If a medical condition becomes widespread, we declare it an epidemic and surprise, surprise, find resources to deal with it. If it is a problem within the purview of the personal services we minimize its existence. Rationalizations such as 'If we take this case seriously we shall have to remove the whole estate' take hold. Yet in reality, if we went to every house in the whole estate we might find poverty but we would not necessarily find neglect. Part of the problem is that poverty and neglect have become synonymous in people's minds. Of course an emotionally healthy family struck by poverty can become so ground down that the pattern of neglect can be discerned. But you can have neglect in a family with two Rolls Royces. The difference is that if you have money the dirt and disorder caused by the apathy and futility may be cleared up by the cleaning lady; the care of children can be given over to a series of au pairs.

The most important reason why neglect is neglected is that right at the core of a neglecting family is an awful intense loneliness. We probably only have a limited capacity to cope with these intense feelings but it brings us up short when we have to face an awful truth. We come into this world alone and go out of it alone.

Neglect cases reveal the weak aspects of our services. Let's take one case to symbolize the problem. Mr A has a psychiatric condition diagnosed by the hospital as untreatable. He therefore ricochets between social services, who see him as a medical problem, and the medical services who see him as a social one. The mother does not attend clinics with her children (Herrenkohl et al 1983). (We have known for a long time we should have mobile clinics, like mobile libraries, to arrive at Mrs A's doorstep.) The children are at the bottom of their class. No one wants to sit next to them because they smell and as Polansky et al (1985) found they 'Make few friends . . . and are isolated' at school. Neglecting families reveal the weak aspects in housing, education, employment, health and social services.

The trouble with neglect cases is that they need help over a long period of time. There are no quick dramatic cures. Professionals seem to be able to co-operate for short bursts of time if there is a superordinate goal. If the child is likely to die, everyone is at the child protection conference. A neglect case is reminiscent of the game of ten green bottles. Gradually the numbers dwindle as every worker discovers more important priorities.

History has also played its part. Neglect was *the* issue in the 1960s. Great debates were initiated to discuss whether there were such things as problem families or were they families with problems. Then in the 1970s the medical profession rediscovered physical abuse. Neglect was tagged on the end. Even today the term 'child abuse and neglect' is used and reveals the attitude that neglect is regarded as 'something else' rather than abuse. The problem is that there is an overlap. Many physically abused children are also the subject of poor child-care but the corollary is not necessarily true.

Violence fascinates. Physical and even sexual abuse are more easily defined. Neglect is insidious and not so easily defined. After all neglect is about sins of omission. Physical abuse is about acts committed. The community's attitude also plays a part. I doubt whether many members of the lay public would suggest that the state should not interfere if a child is being assaulted. But neglect – when do you intervene? When the dirt is an inch high or not until it reaches two inches?

So we all join the grand conspiracy and trot out the usual denials, defences and rationalizations: 'They are a closely knit family and so we should not remove.' 'We mustn't superimpose our middle class standards.' 'We live in the real world; where are we going to find a foster parent for seven children?' 'Anyway the children are happy, just a bit scruffy.' One student at one of my courses described neglect as like an amoeba, with no hard edges. Personally I have always found the definition advanced by Polansky a useful guide.

> Child neglect may be defined as a condition in which a caretaker responsible for the child either deliberately or by extraordinary inattentiveness permits the child to experience avoidable present suffering and/or fails to provide one or more of the ingredients generally deemed essential for developing a person's physical, intellectual and emotional capacities (Polansky 1975).

To examine neglect we need to look at the meeting of the outside and the inside forces.

Outside forces

There is so much in the world that facilitates neglect. Economic, technological and political realities create the stage upon which neglect is acted out. Families tend to come to the attention of government when problems arise. There is little preventive legislation these days and statutory bodies are crisis-orientated. The neglect family that turns up at the office at 4.30 p.m. on a Friday is given 'Just enough help so they can't really make it' (Lally 1984). Television adverts objectify people who are seen as products or consumers. The 'get on your bike' mentality does not pay much regard to the partner and children who are left at home. 'With production as God and the market as a place of worship' (Leach 1990), parenthood is a low priority of the multinational firm that expects a person to jet from breakfast conference to working lunch and an evening meeting across the world. A political system which classically deals with inflation by allowing unemployment to rise devastates the poor and marginally poor. If you are being constantly told that if you try hard enough you can make it, what does it feel like when you never do? Equal opportunities are a myth. Everything out there increases the feelings of impotence and helplessness.

Inside forces
As soon as you start to study neglect, the myth that the children are happy is immediately blown. The neglect can start before birth. The cells of an infant brain may turn out far smaller than is normal if the mother experiences protein deficiency (Vore 1973). The trouble is, neglect does not get publicity. If your skull is broken you appear in the press and in the statistics but neglected children die quietly of respectable illnesses like pneumonia and bronchitis. Neglect is both physically and emotionally lethal. Tonge et al (1975) discovered the mortality rate in neglecting families was 66 per 1000 while the rate in families where there was the same degree of poverty but no neglect was 39 per 1000. The children were found to be more stunted, did less well on IQ tests and had 30 per cent more psychiatric disturbances. Polansky (Polansky et al 1981) notes that because neglected children have to repress so many of their basic needs they find it difficult to empathize with other people's pain so they prove 'peculiarly capable of coldblooded torture or businesslike brutality'. 'Neglected children were four times more likely to be involved in crime' (Tonge et al 1975). Our heartless criminal is therefore likely to have been neglected.

The world for neglected children is a hostile and rejecting one. You huddle with the family behind closed doors. But the huddle is not a warm, nurturing one. The family is caged together for fear of abandonment. You get up in the morning. You pull one sock from the bundle on the floor, then a second, but they are not necessarily yours. In the neglecting home there is no special place for personal, private possessions. Possessions are important in creating self-identity.

Because of my job I travel a lot and I feel as if every three-star hotel bedroom has been painted by the same decorating firm. As the key goes into the door I am a non-person. Not until I've unpacked and got the room into my comfortable state of chaos with *my* possessions do I feel a person again. The neglected child is a non-person. Right from birth they are propped up in the cot with little visual, verbal, intellectual, emotional or physical stimulus. Often it is the eldest child who does the caring.

Sibling-care can be nurturing both ways but not if the parent gives little care and attention to the eldest child who feels unequal to the task. At four or five you are constantly berated for not succeeding. Yet you know that without you, your siblings will be poorly served. So – the martyr is born. Neglected children when they first arrive at school are hyperactive. They run around destroying other children's toys and are unable to concentrate. This is totally understandable. Most of us were blessed with families who fed us in the morning. In the middle of the day food arrived. Before bed there was food. In fact our days had a shape. For neglected children there is no shape. If there is no shape it is difficult to learn. Failure is seen as inevitable. Most skills require children to be able to keep repeating an action until they succeed: for example in riding a bike, or swimming across the pool. Neglected children try once, twice, a few times but as they so fear failure, they seldom succeed.

NEGLECTING PARENTS

If you do not have a map you speed along the motorway not looking to the left or the right. If you do have a map you realize what is around and look at the pretty village nearby. You can see the Gothic arches of the church, discover a new brew of beer at the local pub and also reach your destination.

Polansky (Polansky et al 1981) has given us a map which does not stereotype, but helps us look and *see* and discover what neglect is really all about. To have a chance of helping neglecting families, workers first have to target the apathy, futility and loneliness. Secondly, workers have to grapple with the verbal inaccessibility of the parents. This means that the adults use a lot of words but do not use them to communicate feeling or as a problem-solving process. Thirdly, work has to be concentrated on the repressed anger. Lastly it has to be acknowledged that some clients will cope with their immaturity by impulse-ridden behaviour (Polansky 1986). So according to Polansky (Polansky et al 1981):

1 Neglecting parents are passive withdrawn people lacking in self-expression.
2 They are often disorganized in their lifestyle and childcare. Workers find the parents frustrating as they do not apparently oppose suggestions from workers but do not improve.
3 They have a pervasive conviction about them that nothing is worth doing – as one mother said 'What's the point in cooking supper tonight as tomorrow morning the children will all be hungry again?'
4 Their personal relationships are typified by a desperate clinging but these relationships are superficial, essentially lacking in pleasure and accompanied by loneliness and isolation.
5 The parents have an emotional numbness about them which can sometimes be mistaken for depression or lack of intelligence.
6 Neglecting parents lack competence in many areas of their lives. This is particularly caused by an unwillingness to risk the failure which could result in trying to acquire skills.
7 Often neglecting parents express their anger by being passively aggressive, through hostile compliance. Because they cannot work through their anger, there is a good deal of psychosomatic illness.
8 Neglecting parents infect their workers who pick up the same feelings of futility.
9 There is a tendency for neglecting parents to have an all-or-nothing stereotyped response. They are concrete in their thinking. All this makes them particularly vulnerable to loan sharks (it must be cocktail cabinet rather than shelves).
10 Lastly they have a serious deficiency in their capacity for self-observation, which makes social work difficult.

WORKING WITH NEGLECTING PARENTS

So often agencies have seen the task of helping the neglecting parents as just teaching about child-care, budgeting and hygiene. While the worker is there, often doing most of the work, conditions improve but to the extreme frustration of all those involved, as soon as the worker ceases to visit, the situation quickly deteriorates. The parents have not owned any of the help.

There are no quick cures. But workers stand a greater chance of success if they gently begin by addressing the parents' acute loneliness and anxiety. Polansky (1986) discovered that neglecting parents tended to be more isolated than nurturing parents in comparable families. The neglectful mothers particularly, reported they felt the neighbourhood was less than friendly and unlikely to help them. They had less access to helping networks and were less likely to be part of any informing, helping network than non-neglecting mothers. You have to be prepared to give neighbourliness to receive neighbourliness. As most neglecting parents reject overtures of help they are not part of a neighbourhood network. Neglecting parents are narcissistic. It is their way of cutting off and turning into themselves. To begin to relate means feeling how painfully lonely one is. They mask their feelings, using the children and number of children as buffers against loneliness. The children are extensions of the parents. They are expected to make the parents feel good (Steele 1987). Neglecting mothers cling to their partner, often getting very little from him but it is too awful to countenance life without him (Famulara et al 1986, Herrenkohl et al 1983). It is only when the mother grows inwardly that she can countenance life alone and can acknowledge the damage she experiences in the relationship and perhaps break away from the destructive marriage.

The approach therefore has to be extremely sensitive. Neglecting parents fear the intrusion of the worker who may make them feel emotion and therefore pain. After all they have often only experienced grossly unsatisfying early relationships. All they know is what it is to be ignored or rejected. Certainly they have never been valued as a person, only criticized, manipulated, discounted. Professional workers therefore have to start a long way back and it's easy to confirm negative feelings by accident.

Attentive listening is often the way in. 'No one has ever asked *my* opinion before' can be the breakthrough. Encourage choices and anything that gives self-definition to the clients. It is essential, with people who are so unreliable, to be reliable. Often the deep-seated hostility of the clients is acted out by not answering the door. They feel they are bad people, but the difficulty is that they cannot use words to convey feelings and talk about feelings. There is no magic formula. Sensitive workers have to flay around to create a communication language. Sometimes colours can be useful. Pointing to a colour in the room can be used to help the client describe how he/she feels inside and another colour used to represent how they would like to feel. A colleague recently created a bridge with a client with whom she was making no progress. The worker was tired, exhausted and frustrated. 'Visiting you' she finally exclaimed 'is like going to the bank, drawing out all my paper money, putting it on the floor in front of us and lighting it with a match.' For some reason this comment worked. Things have begun to happen.

Valuing, reaching out and touching the loneliness and offering care and concern seems to work. Children use transitional objects to test things out before they approach their parents and then the outside world. Neglecting parents, because their own parents were so uncaring and hostile, need to test things out with the worker. Because they are concrete people there have to be concrete offers of help. But any material aid has to be given in a way that tops up the parents. The children need shoes, but help has to be offered in a way that makes the parents feel better and builds up the way they feel about being parents.

Family aids, special home helps or home carers are particularly valuable. But social workers and ancillaries must be jointly supervised, otherwise the clients will keep everyone impotent by playing them off against each other. The mother needs to be re-mothered, to have fun in an incredibly miserable life. The anxiety makes neglecting parents slip into safe fantasy worlds which can be television, alcohol or drugs (Famulara et al 1986). Their apparent depression and numbness is often mistaken for laziness, irresponsibility or even lack of intelligence. They escape their anxieties by living for the present. Workers have to recognize the parents are anxious about things that would not provoke anxiety in themselves and may not be anxious about something the worker feels they *should* be anxious about: for example, not paying the rent.

It is important to discover what it is that is keeping the parent immobile and unable to use help. Is it a profound feeling that 'I don't deserve anything better so there's no point in trying'? Are they so angry that they have to destroy any signs of progress? Do they face the dilemma that if they matured they would have to face the world and cope?

Often clients are kept locked into their own problems because neglecting households become the responsibility of so many agencies. The key worker concept should be brought in from its success with physical abuse. Parents do not have to grow when they can manipulate a whole string of professionals. Statutory responsibilities can all be operated through one key worker.

This worker has to find some leverage that will move the situation. It may be the setting of limits. Any use of authority has to be competent, unexploitive, supportive and helpful. Most neglecting parents have only experienced authority as punitive, controlling and exploitive. There has to be some movement. Just propping up the family, which is offering nothing to the children, is not good practice and is damaging to the children.

A final point. As long ago as 1978 Garbarino and Sherman said 'Socially impoverished families may be particularly vulnerable to socially impoverished environments.' So the mobilization of friendly networks and volunteers can make a real difference. However, to start with, a good deal of support and encouragement from professionals is required, as neglecting families are so hostile and manipulative.

Working with neglecting mothers

Groups offer a ray of hope. Neglecting mothers really do seem able to use groups positively. Two workers are needed for the mothers' group and two for the children's group. To start with, the mother will need much individual work, as groups have not been comfortable experiences. She may have failed at school and work. Transport has to be laid on as in their chaotic world they will not make it under their own steam. The person driving the car or bus to pick up parent and child needs to be incredibly positive: the sort of person who has the mother's coat on and down the stairs and in the car before she has finished telling the reasons why she and the child are not coming. To wait for self-motivation means work will never get started.

Groups meet so many needs. They offer straight respite from a grey burdensome life. They offer a first place to have fun. To begin with children may keep running in, destroying the mothers' group, but as soon as a mother feels more comfortable her children can begin to use their group. The mothers' group helps the female partner learn she is not the only one with problems. In fact she may have something to offer a fellow member to solve her difficulties.

The group gives shape to a shapeless existence. It provides a purpose for washing your hair. Workers can give care in an acceptable way, by providing fun, food and pleasantly set out cups of tea. Food is very important. In an isolated world networks can be built up, and practical lessons in communicating and giving positive strokes to others. What's more difficult is learning how to receive positive strokes.

A range of practical activities have been found valuable. Many mothers do not know *how* to play with their children. They see the children playing and take over the game with yells of joy. It's a very new experience, playing. Paradox can be useful. At the beginning only five minutes is allowed for the mother to play *with* her children. The worker initiates the game with mother and child. As it's only for five minutes the mother can bear it. She is frightened. As she learns actually to enjoy the game – and her child – the time limit is lengthened. To start with the mother can only play *as* a child not *with* a child.

There can be activities such as cooking and outside lectures. The worker may be most useful by genuinely failing at some of the activities (whatever stuffed toy I made, be it a rabbit, toy elephant, always collapsed as the legs spread out and slowly fell to the floor). If the worker can teach how to cope with failure and how still to feel good about yourself, a very worthwhile lesson has been learnt. Discussion groups around marital problems, care of children, use of services, come later in the programme. (There is a whole battery of self-esteem exercises in McGuire and Priestley (1991) which can be adapted for neglectful mothers.)

Working with neglecting fathers/cohabitees

Face-to-face work seems to work best with neglecting fathers and cohabitees. Workers have to remember that behind the heavy facade of repressed hostility and irresponsibility is an acute anxiety. The man's feelings, problems and interests have to be focused upon. He usually has little interest in homemaking. He certainly doesn't take his female partner with him when he goes out. He's often the sort of man who is alone in a crowded pub. Frequently he is even more disorganized than his wife and hooked on cigarettes, beer or drugs for instant satisfaction. It's not easy to track down the male client. As the worker comes through the front door he goes out of the back door. The child protection conference team tend to focus their whole interest on mother and children. He feels a spare part and wants to keep it that way (Garbarino and Sherman 1980). However workers who can mesh in with the fear and feeling of fright, who don't lecture and berate, have a good chance of beginning work. Fathers and cohabitees are often as in need of care as the children and the mother.

Games

Neglectful parents are often brilliant games players. They hook us into games that make us impotent and keep us from intruding lest we make them feel and develop emotionally. Here are a few we have to learn to recognize.

Look how hard I'm trying

The parents try to convince us they are co-operating. 'I did what you suggested social worker, now look what a mess I'm in. You sort it all out, it's now your problem and your fault.'

'Yes but!'

Whatever the worker suggests the reply is 'Yes, I'd love to agree to do X but ...'. But there is always an excuse why something cannot possibly work.

I'm stupid

'I'm stupid so you can't expect me to do or go anywhere, you do it for me!'

You and the DHSS fight

The worker spends all the time fighting agencies on the parents' behalf while they remain static, not moving or changing in any way.

Menacing demands
'If you don't do what I want I'll leave the kids on your doorstep/ abandon them/ batter them!'

Your're not as good as the last worker
The constant unfavourable comparison with the last worker not only makes the present worker feel impotent but is a way to manipulate the worker into meeting a client's unreasonable demands.

You're wonderful
'You're the first worker who's ever understood me!' This approach keeps the worker from setting limits and making demands for fear of losing a 'beautiful relationship'.

Continuing practical problems
The worker feels that once the practical problems are solved she can get down to some really useful work. But she never can as a new crop of crises keep emerging.

The hidden agreement
The neglectful parent turns up at the office at 4.30 p.m. on a Friday and is given, on demand, money to last the weekend. Clients and worker make an unwritten unconscious contract: 'If you don't turn up too often you can have another grant in a few weeks time.' The process becomes a repeated trap. Both sides are avoiding the issues. The worker, feeling depressed and futile about the whole case, reassures herself that at least she's doing something 'constructive'.

WORKING WITH NEGLECTED CHILDREN

Face-to-face work with neglected children has to begin as early as possible. Years of isolation, social and emotional, may lead to neglected children building up their defences. As Polansky says (Polansky et al 1981) 'they turn mean' and help given when ten or eleven may be too late.

Before neglected children can join a group they need a great deal of individual work. They need exercises that help them see themselves as separate people in their own right and not just part of a huddle. Games that build up self-confidence, confirming that the world is not a hostile place are useful. (See Chapter 8.) The regular monitoring services of the community physician and health visitor are necessary. When children are dressed it is easy to miss that they may be seriously underweight.

Above all, neglected children need to be treated as children, especially the eldest child who may have shouldered all the household responsibilities. Such a child may need to regress and become totally irresponsible and dependent. This of course has to be meshed in with work with the parents (otherwise no children will be cared for!) Small successes are essential and situations should be provided that offer stimulation: social, intellectual and emotional. Special tutoring may be required as the neglected child hasn't been given the necessary basics to benefit from class learning. Social skills training is essential as neglected children have always had to grab and demand for themselves so they have little idea of co-operative play. This then makes them unpopular with other children, further deepening their feelings of isolation. Smaller children may have to start by being taught routines, boundaries and basic habits such as toilet training, at the family centre.

This is where male workers come into their own, whether it is in individual, group work or in being part of a team at a family centre. So often, according to Polansky (Polansky et al 1981) neglected children 'spoke less often to their fathers, interacted less positively with them and initiated fewer physical contacts with them.' In fact the fathers were characterized by their low rates of positive responses and failure to comply with their children's requests. Male workers can therefore offer a male model and show that men can have feelings and can relate.

CHILD PROTECTION CONFERENCES

Because neglecting families have so many problems, a large number of agencies tend to be involved. This is a real challenge to those chairing child protection conferences. It is so easy to lose focus and purpose. Building on the work of Day

Table 5.1

Type of neglect	Peter	John	Anne	Tracy	
Nutritional	2	2	1	1	
Physical	5	1	1	1	1 Low
Emotional	2	2	2	1	5 High
Developmental	2	1	2	2	
Protection	3	2	2	1	

Table 5.2

Peter Type of neglect	More	Less
Nutritional	protein foods	sweets
Physical	warm clothing	wet beds
Emotional	listening to	taking the mick re. big ears
Developmental	stimulation	attention to size
Protection	consistent limits	unsupervised play
Other		

(1983) I would suggest the strategy of attaching to the wall two large sheets of paper. On the first, as shown in Table 5.1, are written the areas of child development. Any categories agreeable to the conference can be used. Each child is then rated on a five-point range. This at least means all the members of the conference have to look individually at each child. So often children of neglecting families are seen as a bunch. If the rating is low then the team has to see if services can be provided to supplement what the parents are offering. If services cannot be provided, then the next question to be considered is, 'Should the children remain at home?'

The second sheet, (see Table 5.2), looks at the same areas again. The whole conference has to agree on one narrow area to target in each section – for instance 'more protein, less sweets' – until the next case discussion. By beaming down on narrowly defined objectives in each area there is a chance of success. With neglecting families both workers and the family need small but measurable successes.

CONCLUSION

When you consider the number of inquiry reports that have been about neglected children, for instance Lucy Gates (1982), Steven Meurs (1975), Malcolm Page (1981), Doreen Mason (1989), it is a cruel twist of fate that we still neglect neglect. Neglect is at the heart of so many of the problems that perplex us and cost the community so much in personal and financial terms.

B
THE WORKER

6 The Worker

When three-inch high headlines in the press are castigating a professional for mishandling a case of child abuse, the rest of us have two major responses. The first is a humble feeling which can be summed up by 'It could be me!' The second, if we are absolutely honest, is a puzzled range of questions as to why that worker behaved in the way she/he did. The conundrum becomes more entangled when we know the worker personally to be skilful, concerned and experienced. Perhaps the comment in the Kimberley Carlile report (1987) says it all. The worker was left 'haunted at the end by incomprehension – why had he not taken steps that seem so obvious to him in retrospect?'

There are at least five powerful phenomena that can attack us as soon as we start to handle a child abuse case and lead us to performing at a lower level than our professional competence.

PICKUP

As soon as we begin to work with the feelings of abusing families we get sucked in by the family system and become vulnerable. Often we are surprised at the strength and conflict of the feelings involved. In reality we are knocked off balance. The feelings get to us and we lose our professional cool. So often workers are too ashamed to talk about these feelings as they consider them to be the very antithesis of what is regarded as professional. After all many agencies have updated business models based 'on male dominated institutions in commercial life. Such climates tend to emphasise some of the major stereotypical characteristics of male psychology, competitiveness, self-sufficiency, over reliance on logic and an under-valuing of the validity of feeling, or worse, a belief that feelings demonstrate incompetence or weakness' (Morrison 1990).

It would be bad enough if the feelings just hit head on, but those we pick up are ambivalent. First there is the mixture of *omnipotence and impotence*. We begin to feel that if we try hard enough we should be able to protect all children in our area and be omnipotent. Yet with our heads we know that many abusing parents are so badly damaged that even if we set up a twenty four hour vigil they would still find a way of damaging their children. The trouble is that so often the lay public is misled. After each tragedy some local or national politician reassures the public through the media that all will now be all right because procedures have been tightened up. What the public has to face is that a professional can do all that anyone can expect and follow the guidelines completely and still a child may die. A death does not automatically mean a professional was at fault.

The other side of omnipotence is *impotence*. Child abuse work makes us feel powerless. We quickly realize that one visit is not going to undo years of damaging experiences. We feel de-skilled and it's easy to chase rainbows and make registers, procedures and policies into talismans. Procedures can sharpen practice and thus protect more children but we cannot protect all children.

The next pair of feelings are *anger and guilt*. Anger wells up in the worker when after so much work the parents let us down: anger with ourselves that we have become mesmerized by all the pain inside the parent so that we've not seen the hurt of the child; anger that now our work will be exposed in minute detail to the whole community. After all, it is easy to be critical with the benefit of hindsight and in perfect conditions. Most of us, however, visit unwilling clients when the alsatian is barking, water is seeping down the walls of the house and it is the end of a horrendous day. We are also angry that a child or a baby should have experienced hurt at the hands of the very people who should be protective.

Mixed with the anger is the *guilt*: guilt that we should have listened more, especially to the child; guilt that we did not do all the obvious things. We then take on all the guilt and can so easily become the battered worker.

The last pair of feelings are *depression and accusation*. At the back of the Kimberley Carlile report (1987) there is a list of child abuse inquiries. What is interesting about this list is that the largest number of cases were those in which there was no statutory order. This emphasizes the point that most child abuse situations are those that could be called 'fuzzy'. In a way the 'hairy' cases will get the attention they deserve but the ones that cause the strain are those that everybody knows about, but feels it is impossible to do anything constructive.

These are the cases that can drift and then suddenly erupt. The difficulty is that before the explosion we become bored because they have dragged on for so long, draining us dry. We feel overwhelmed and start to blame. We blame lack of resources – quite rightly, as many of the basic requirements needed to achieve success in child abuse are still not available for each case; for example, day centres, night nurseries and travelling medical services. But even if we had all the resources in the world, child abuse cases would still make us feel drained, scapegoated and under-supported.

If we put all feelings together (see Figure 6.1) all the emotion flows through us and we become the human animal we are. We become impotent: stuck like a rabbit caught in the headlights of a car (Moore 1982). We present to the world a petrified stance that can resemble an uncaring negligence.

LEARNED HELPLESSNESS

The next powerful phenomenon is learned helplessness. Martin Seligman experimented with dogs. He put them in cages and put through the cage irregular electric shocks. They had to be irregular because when we come to look at humans, we are better at coping with trauma when we know it is going to happen (Seligman 1975). In the original experiments after a brief period of trying to escape the animals just flopped to the floor and didn't make an attempt to get out even when the

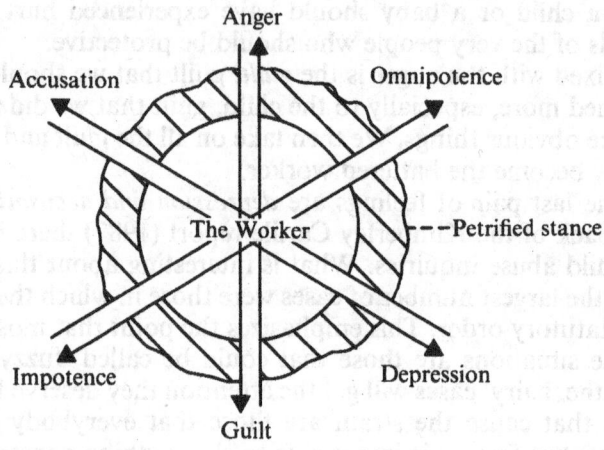

Figure 6.1

door of the cage was opened. They had to be dragged out by the experimenters.

Seligman then observed human beings and came up with the theory that if people are put into situations that they fear are inescapable then their human motivation becomes sapped; their desire to initiate action, solve problems and overcome obstacles all declines. Our very ability to perceive success is undermined. We fear we have lost control over our lives even if in fact we have not. We may resist offers of help even if 'someone with power to intervene tries to do so' (Doyle 1990). We experience that awful combination of depression, anger and anxiety which constitutes learned helplessness.

The trouble with this state is that it is infectious. Workers catch it too! We don't ask the right questions. We feel unable to confront and experience awful feelings of tedium and failure. This is when cases start to drift. Even at the child protection conference everyone is locked into learned helplessness and feels unable to take positive action.

VICTIM/VICTIMIZER SYNDROME

Even more complicated is the victim/victimizer situation. This is when we become completely confused by what we observe and misread the signs from the children.

Understanding what happens in abusive families becomes clearer when we remember in 1973 Jan Eric Olsen and his friend held hostage four employees of the Svergis Kredit Bank in Stockholm (Strenz 1980). In fact the siege lasted for 131 hours. Fortunately there was an American psychiatrist, Ocberg, in the city and he asked the police if he could monitor the situation. He predicted correctly that after 72 hours a powerful bond would be forged between the victims and the victimizers: so powerful that the hostages during their captivity negotiated on behalf of the bank robbers and then protected them from the guns of the police at the end of the siege by walking in front of the robbers. Further, they refused to give evidence and one hostage later divorced her husband to marry one of the victimizers (Wardlaw 1982). This experience helps to explain why a child feeling helpless in the hands of a parent on whom his or her life depends, has a powerful desire to breathe into the parents moral values and human qualities which will make survival more likely. Furthermore when you are totally helpless and the parent has all the power, to identify with the parent can relieve feelings of helplessness. During the 1939/45 war some long-standing prisoners in concentration camps took pride in copying the verbal and physical aggression of the guards towards fellow prisoners and would try to make SS uniforms for themselves (Bettleheim 1979).

Intermeshed with this phenomenon is the way humans respond to physical attacks upon them. If one is unfortunate enough to be mugged one's first reaction is disbelief. If the attacker stays, many victims go through a period of psychological infantilism, appeasing the attacker. After it is all over they experience a mixture of anger, guilt and self-accusation. They shouldn't have been in the street at that time!

We go through the same pattern with regard to abuse. In the first stage, we don't want to believe that this client could do such a thing. In the second stage we become too dependent upon procedures. We become immobile – let's just monitor the case! And after it's all over the feelings of anger, guilt and self-accusation swamp us, so we perform badly at the inquiry.

Understanding the effects of victim/victimizer syndrome has helped us understand why children give us such wrong clues. It is easy for an inexperienced worker to visit a family and to misread the clinging of a child to a parent as affection. Abused children often split off from the abuse of the previous night and live for the moment so a child is seen playing happily on the floor. If the worker does not relate in a face-to-face way with the child, it is easy to assume that all is well.

Workers can reassure themselves the child is protected if there is a good parent. Yet we know there is nothing more sure to make a person impotent than a 'good' interrogator alternating with a 'bad' one. An abused child is put into this position time and time again especially as so many abusive parents can have periods when they are quite kind to their children. It is not therefore surprising that abused children become impotent and passively accept what happens to them. This in turn makes the worker impotent too.

DOMINANT IDEAS

The power of dominant ideas can kill (Moore 1984). They can skew our performance. To explain the phenomenon, imagine you are at the theatre. From your seat in the front row of the stalls you see the dancing and hear the singing. But as soon as the star appears you only have eyes for her. No longer do you see or hear the bit parts. This is the trouble with dominant ideas. In themselves they are good ideas but they drive everything else out of the way. To illustrate the point let us have a look at a few:

Classification
Because a case is, for instance, classified as a housing case, no-one thinks of child abuse. Lester Chapman (1979) died because the 'housing' label on the case blinded the workers and they couldn't see the physical and emotional abuse that was happening to the child.

Frozen watchfulness
The slides shown to us on qualifying courses, depicting frozen watchfulness in abused children, are so powerful that we assume all abused children will behave in a cowed way. Abused children may instead be destructive, angry and difficult. Then workers see the child as having the problem, instead of being abused.

Removal as the last resort

This idea can become so dominant that in spite of a searching assessment we do not use the information we have gathered. We go through the motions of rehabilitation, leaving the child in an abusive situation, when instead we should be thinking of removal as the first resort in some cases.

Stereotyping

There can be positive as well as negative stereotyping. Because Mrs Henry (Tyra Henry Report 1987) was a grandmother, black and a woman, the worker got caught up in the precept that grandmothers cope, black women cope, women cope. Mrs Henry was therefore put by the workers into a situation where no person could be expected to cope. There was acute poverty, bad housing and Mrs Henry was going through a period of deep mourning. Positive stereotyping can skew the whole situation.

Fostering

Fostering can become a dominant idea. It has the added advantage of being cheaper than residential care. However, a fostering situation may be too emotive for an abused child. He/she may not be ready for the natural focus of two adults. What the child may need is the more neutral environment of a good, well-run and sensitive small children's home, but if fostering is the immediate and dominating response, we do not set up such establishments as the need is not seen. Instead we face the numerous breakdowns in foster care.

Robert Dingwall (Dingwall et al 1983) has given us a host of dominant ideas. Love is one. Because parents genuinely love their children we assume they cannot be abusive. Because parents are co-operating, the assumption is that they are changing. He also challenges us to improve our practice with violent clients. Workers should not be put at risk. Joint visiting is required as is training in recognizing and working with anger and irrational hostility.

Lastly Dingwall reminds us that we need to develop skills in three areas: first, coping with clients who are articulate and able to use all the available resources. For example, we visit and the lawyer is sitting with the parents while we complete our investigation. Secondly, Dingwall challenges us on our lack of skills in working with ethnic groups and thirdly, that in paying extra attention to the mentally ill or the parent with learning difficulties we miss the effects upon the child.

Now to the last of our powerful phenomena:

BURNOUT

Until a few years ago it was convenient for management to believe burnout was something that only occurred with poor workers. In fact it is the opposite (Pines et al 1981). Sadly there is still a stigma attached to burnout. Instead, it should be seen as a natural and normal hazard of the job. Burnout is likely to occur two to two-and-a-half years after qualifying and will keep reoccurring, if we are any good, throughout our careers. Those who do not work with feelings or outreach to clients will never get burnout! What we have to learn is how to use our burnout to move on and become a better worker.

A definition
Pines (Pines et al 1981) describes burnout as a state of mind that frequently afflicts individuals who work with other people and those who pour in much more than they get back from their clients, supervisors and colleagues.

> It is accompanied by an array of symptoms that include a general malaise, emotional, physical and psychological fatigue: feelings of helplessness, hopelessness and a lack of enthusiasm about work and even about life in general. It is insidious in that it usually does not occur as a result of one or two traumatic events but sneaks up through an erosion of the spirit.

The trouble with burnout is that we start to lose concern for our clients. We do not see the clues. We start to stereotype and behave in routinized ways, feeling too tired to see, hear or take action. This response is naturally disastrous for child abuse.

Why child abuse causes burnout
Child abuse work is particularly likely to cause burnout. As we get caught up with abusing parents, the anger, the hate and sadness in us is resurrected. Abusive parents have to test out

our indestructibility and clients need to be sure that we will not retaliate. In order to protect a child we have to keep returning to situations where we feel impotent and de-skilled. Our own uncomfortable childhood experiences may be brought to the surface again as abusing parents try to manipulate and control us. Perhaps worse, is having to face that in some situations we do not have the skills or the knowledge to change anything at all.

Child abuse is about making decisions. The trouble is we never know what would have happened if, for instance, we had left the child at home. Constantly we are caught in impossible conflicts. If we meet the needs of the child, the mentally ill mother will be devastated. Often the balancing act of trying to respond to everyone in the family is not successful. Things become even more perilous when a community swings from demanding that the welfare of the child is paramount, to the stance that the integrity and sanctity of the family must be kept intact at all costs. Often it is impossible to find the middle ground.

I have stressed already that the interdisciplinary approach is essential in child protection. This means we are constantly entering into other professions' territories. This in itself is stressful. To add to our problems, because there is so much anger ricocheting around, the professional team can get caught in what Furniss (1991) calls 'conflict by proxy' and 'then fight family battles inside the professional group'.

We do not work on a desert island. We are members of teams and often of large organizations. Unconstructive wrangles can go on within a team which can often be a team in name but not in fact. Often we do not work as a team but as a number of lone hedgehogs. This isolation can be stressful. Large open-plan offices may meet some needs but certainly do not provide the privacy to think through a case. In fact the noise level in these offices is often quite high. All of this affects our performance (Cox 1978). There is additional stress if the general atmosphere is not supportive, valuing, challenging or does not make us feel we belong and have an identity of competence. Hatchett (1991) reported that in a community care survey 40 per cent of field workers said they only saw the director 'once a year or less' and 'an incredible 40 per cent said never'. Such an ambience creates burnout.

SUPERVISION

Because of everything that has already been spelt out, supervision is essential in child abuse work: for the sake of the clients, the worker and the agency. The problem is that management skills have become more important than supervisory skills. I would go so far as to say it is dangerous for a worker to carry a child abuse case if regular, sensitive, structured, scheduled supervision is not given.

Kadushin (1976) has suggested supervision may be seen as a three-sided triangle. Unless all three sides are included the whole construct collapses. The three aspects are administrative, educative and supportive.

Both parties need to share their expectations of supervision and contract to prepare beforehand and write up decisions, areas covered and themes that emerged in the session.

Administrative supervision

If imagination is used, administrative supervision can not only ensure the agency's policies, priorities, and philosophies are put into practice but can also tell us, sometimes quicker than other aspects of supervision, what is happening with a case. If we start to carry out guidelines in an unthinking, rigid, inflexible way it may show that we have acute fear and anxiety about a particular case. If rules are ignored, is it a sign we are getting sucked in and have over-identified with one of the parents? Slack administration can mean the victim inside us is colluding with the victim part of a client. Unwillingness to abide by rules may be because we are afraid to confront a situation. We need supervision to make us aware.

Educative supervision

Child abuse is a fast-growing area. We need constantly to be challenged so that we update and develop our skills and understanding. It is easy to get bored with some of our ongoing cases of neglect. Supervisors need to help us look at new ways of handling things. Turn the case upside down and one can come at it in an entirely new way. Supervisors need to create opportunities for achievement and recognition as Herzberg (1968) states: 'These are the best motivators but cannot just be tackled once but constantly'. So to grow, supervisors and supervisees need to discover how the worker learns, not in a broad conceptual framework, but practically. Is the worker for instance a plodder, an inspirational leaper or an absorber? Does the worker learn through her eyes or through her ears? The supervisor then has to adapt his or her approach to meet the educative needs of the worker and discover what stage of learning the worker is at. A supervisor is a teacher, an educator.

Supportive supervision
Supportive supervision is vital; it is what keeps us going. So much of child abuse work is slow slog. It is not support versus the agency but within it, creating the atmosphere within the session of mutual trust and respect, which fosters critical discussion and honest evaluation. The supervisor should be a mentor and not a tormentor. We need our work valued and to be shown how we can use success in one case to help another one.

Managers
Managers can only supervise if they have been trained for the task. They can only supervise if they too are supervised. Otherwise the pain and feelings are locked between supervisor and supervisee and collusion results. One difficulty is that so many managers feel under siege themselves, trying to protect services from attack and cut corners to survive. Part of the problem is a myth has taken hold that the higher up the hierarchy you go, the less you need supervision. The opposite is true. Without comprehensive supervision workers and the organization can get burnt out. Supervision is one of the best antidotes to burnout.

Gender issues
Gender issues have to be addressed in supervision – particularly if the case is one of child sexual abuse. If the supervisor is a man and the worker is a woman the power structure of the abuse is recreated. This is particularly painful if the worker was herself abused. As it is estimated 25–40 per cent of workers have experienced some form of abuse this is a real possibility (Morrison 1990). Men and women tend to respond to painful feelings differently. Without stereotyping, men have a tendency to turn their painful feelings outwards and women turn their feelings inwards. The possibility of crossed lines is

therefore very likely, with the woman worker feeling the male supervisor doesn't understand and is hard-hearted and the male supervisor, irritated by the tears of the woman, feeling she is making a meal of the whole situation. To add to the complexity of the supervision, we have to acknowledge men and women use words very differently. According to Tannen (1990) women tend to identify with and stay with another woman if they feel intensely. Men tend to look for solutions. We have to understand 'genderlect' if there are not to be crossed wires and the woman worker is not to finish the supervision session feeling victimized, invalidated and powerless like the sexually abused child. Painful situations can cause flashbacks with the woman worker remembering parts of the child's experiences in her intimate moments and putting her off sex with her own partner.

If it is a female supervisor and a male worker equally complex issues can arise. The situation could reflect his abuse by his mother and he feels smothered and belittled. His socialization makes the male worker ensure he is *not* going to be dominated. He may cover this up by playing the role of 'little boy lost' or 'mum knows best', either of which will divert attention away from the case. Idealization of the mother role may ensure the role of the female partner in the abuse is not evaluated.

If it is a male supervisor and a male worker the game of 'we are all men of the world' can begin and women and children become objectified: 'After all, girls ask for it'. If it is a woman supervisor and a woman worker the two can unite and play the game of 'all men are bastards', 'what else do you expect?' and scapegoat the male client. This again avoids looking at the female partner as all women are either made madonnas or child protective amazons.

Games
It is not only clients who play games. If we unconsciously start to play games with our supervisors we have blocked a process which is meant to be developmental, supportive and can even be invigorating. Some of the well known games are:

Two versus the agency
We take a casual throwaway line, say about form filling, and exploit it. 'What's really important is face-to-face work as you

said; these forms are just keeping administrative section in a job.' After this it is difficult for the supervisor to insist on completion of forms.

Let me do my own thing
The worker insists he or she can only do their best work if given plenty of space. This makes the supervisor impotent, afraid of being accused of curbing professional autonomy.

You're wonderful!
The supervisee flatters the supervisor by saying how valuable the supervision sessions are. 'No-one has given me such valuable sessions.' This makes it difficult for the supervisor to challenge, lest the good worker relationship is lost. Managers seldom have warm feedbacks so he/she doesn't want to lose out on this one.

Treat me, don't beat me
The worker regales the supervisor with so many personal problems there isn't time to look at client records. Anyway the supervisor would feel dreadful pressing the worker about painful work situations when they have so many personal problems. This is when the supervisor has to be careful not to slip into a therapy role. The task of the supervisor is to help the worker with the professional task. Any personal understanding that may accrue through this process is purely a bonus. One cannot mix the role of supervisor and therapist.

Supervision is not for friends
If the supervisor has been promoted from within the group the worker tries to make the supervisor impotent by recounting and reminding of past adventures. This subtly implies that the new senior cannot expect to play the boss as the worker knows too much about him.

I know Kempe better than you
This game is particularly powerful if the supervisor has come from a different specialism. The worker makes it clear that supervision cannot be expected from someone who knows so much less about child abuse. Of course the skills of supervision are quite different from knowledge of the subject.

I'm more in touch
The worker attempts to make the supervisor impotent by suggesting the worker is more in touch with here-and-now problems: 'After all you haven't practised for years – it's not like it was in *your* day.'

I have a little list!
This worker feeds the supervisor with interesting discussion issues. The session ends having been a fascinating seminar but with cases not supervised.

It's all useless!
'Nothing works in this county. It may have worked in your last area but this is Blanktown, it won't work here!'

Heading off criticism
The worker bursts into tears at the beginning of the session and confesses all. She/he has made a terrible mess of things. The supervisor starts to comfort her and begins to say 'It's not as bad as you think – cheer up.' Both are now hooked because it is bad but now the situation has been minimized.

What would you do!
If the supervisor is tricked into actually giving advice the knockdown punch comes in the second round: 'I did what you said and it didn't work!'

RACISM

Finally of crucial importance, racism must be addressed and challenged. Only then can an appropriate service be offered to black families who abuse. David Divine* writes:

Repeatedly white professionals are the beneficiaries of information, insight, experience, outcomes of pain felt by black people – both lay and professional – occasioned by a society which allocates worth on the basis of skin colour. In my written response to a request to address the Jasmine Beckford Inquiry (1985) I stated that there were two major sources of

---

*David Divine is Assistant Director, Central Council for Education and Training in Social Work.

information about black people utilized by practitioners in making decisions about black people:

(i) research on black people (usually 'problem' centred) carried out by white academics and
(ii) 'professional' commentary on black people who, usually through some misfortune or other come to the attention of social services. It is the academic's/practitioner's interpretation of the family's difficulty which is canvassed and which is eventually found in local government statistics, not that of the families' involved (Divine 1985).

> The information gleaned from the above sources is essentially flawed and feeds – and even more dangerously, provides 'academic credibility' to – popular stereotypes about black people which are already given the status 'fact'. When such mis-information is used as background to decision making then one can only expect problems regarding communication, faulty decision-making and distress to the consumer (Divine 1982/3).

The content of the quote is still accurate some six years later although an increasing number of texts produced by blacks on the complicated multifaceted nature of life in the black communities are seeing the light of day. The potential shape of black and white dialogue over the past several hundred years has been corroded by white hegemony. The content of the actual dialogue is characterized by the perceived intrinsic inferiority of blacks to whites. The institutionalization of the latter perception was enshrined for the first time by Elizabeth I in 1596 and again in 1601 when she issued a Privy Council directive which attempted to expel all black people from Britain. This institutionalized perception is pervasive today in black and white contact which needs to be acknowledged and reflected upon by both parties and decisions taken as to whether attempts will be made to work through them as far as an individual can, or whether we will allow our history and our present reality to preclude real dialogue.

Audrey Lorde, a prominent black woman writer answers this question in a poignant letter to a white sister stating the following:

> I had decided never again to speak to white women about racism. I felt it was wasted energy, because of their destructive guilt and defensiveness, and because whatever I had to say might better be

said by white women to one another, at far less emotional cost to the speaker. and probably with a better hearing. This letter attempts to break this silence.

I would like not to have to destroy you in my consciousness. So as a sister. . . .I ask you to speak to my perceptions (Lorde 1981).

In attempting to 'break this silence' in the field of social service provision to black people we need to remind ourselves of its history and perceived impact. We cannot begin to understand the complexity of black family functioning and gain insight into when some of its forms malfunction, without a grasp of the facts of racism. 'The black family socialises children to be able to cope with the realities of the black community and at the same time, to deal with prejudice and discrimination from the larger culture which singularly affects them' (Gary 1974). The history of social services provision to black people in Britain has ranged from a 'like it or lump it' approach at best to one of direct discrimination resulting in unnecessary suffering and, some would argue, death at its worst. This is not to deny the exceptional practice which was positive but the general pattern as perceived by the customer and significant numbers of conscious black professionals in the business was that the impact of social services on the black recipient was destructive. Institutional racism permeates social services provisions in that it occurs 'whenever individuals in carrying out the routine practices of their employment or institution produce outcomes which *in their effect* discriminate against members of black and minority ethnic groups' (Husband 1991). Husband continues: even 'nice people can be accused of being culpable of participating in generating racist outcomes.'

It is true to say that over the past decade it could be argued that there has been a significant increase in the profile of ideas about service delivery to black people and that increased numbers of black people appear to be coming into the 'caring' professions as practitioners and managers. A word of caution however is needed in making a direct equation of increased profile and increased black professional participation with automatic improvement in service delivery to black people.

> These persons have themselves been trained in white institutions, been required to learn and demonstrate competence in essentially white conceptions of knowledge and practice and have been promoted within a white system. For some their 'professionalism'

will have resulted in an identification with the dominant institutional values. All black managers will be confronted with the political necessity of working through, if not entirely within, the institutions' professional values. The ideology of professionalism within social work practice must be recognised as an important factor of institutional racism' (Husband 1991).

What substantive improvement there has been of direct benefit to black consumers is debatable. That is not to say there has not been improvement. There demonstrably has been in certain areas. It simply means we need to catalogue what changes are professed to have occurred and subject them to scrutiny using the customer and the wider black communities as a partner in that evaluation.

* * *

CONCLUSION

Child abuse work is not child's play. It is stressful and challenging. We have to take the responsibility of demanding supervision and working positively with our burnout and racism. Then child protection can be rewarding, interesting and even stimulating.

7 A Misassessment of Black Families in Child Abuse Work

*Emmanuel Okine**

The investigation and assessment of black children and their families is a complex and controversial issue for social workers and their managers. The subject, in my opinion cannot be isolated from the dynamics of race, and racism, nor from other aspects of discrimination such as gender, class, age, sexuality and differently abled people. These factors are entrenched realities of social work practice with families, both black and white, in the twentieth century. However, what has always emerged from my experience is that the needs of black families are too often viewed as 'the same' as for white families. The result is that some black families can find social work intervention to be an overzealous intrusion and a marginalization of black family life through a colour-blind approach. This viewpoint has the effect of social workers making a misassessment of child abuse, possibly with subsequent devastating outcomes for children and families. This three-way relationship can have a demoralizing impact upon child protection workers conscious about the disproportionate numbers of black children in care, yet unable to change or challenge preconceived ideas and behaviour in themselves or the agencies which they represent.

---

* Emmanuel Okine is Probation Officer with Inner London Probation Service and a former social worker with Manchester, Derbyshire and Tameside Social Services.

As a black worker and a former child protection social worker with other experiences in a long-term child care team, the misassessment of child abuse work with black families has been a major concern to me on both a personal and a professional level for many years. This is mainly because practitioners and managers do not accept the need to assess black families within the context of the political, social and economic arena. Throughout a period of practice that exceeds eleven years and includes academic studies, it is a reality that the literature on the subject is both sparse and confusing. Most workers, black and white, find the material available conflicting and misleading. Increasingly, and prior to the introduction of the Children Act, there has been wide acknowledgement that the needs of black children and their families have gone unaddressed in assessment processes.

There are several often complex reasons for this, but one possible explanation is that within the framework of assessments made by social workers of abusing black families, there is no recognition of racism, that it exists and is alive within British society. Less significantly, there is no real commitment to the view that the issues of anti-discriminatory practice apply centrally to the assessment process. When workers have ignored these issues, which are fundamental to the principles of good practice, they not only fail themselves, but also contribute to the perpetuation of racism and family breakdown in an institutionalized format. I would lend great weight to the view that without the benefit of an objective assessment, a full and professional investigation in child abuse work cannot be achieved.

The main arguments that lead me to this view are that the policy and practice of a local authority are institutionally based. As racism is an endemic feature of our society, a significant proportion of social workers are reinforcing a negative conception of black families from a notional mode of superiority. A black individual and family can be perceived in contrasting ways, as inferior and unable to cope, or at worst, as so resourceful that it seems unnecessary for the social worker to offer departmental services. Also contributing to this spiral of negativity can be the geographical location of black families which contribute significantly to what services they receive and how they receive them.

The misassessment of black children and their families, has

its roots in a Eurocentric perspective of black children and family life that is judgemental in essence. It is racially biased, stereotypical in presence, and frequently full of mythology. Nobody would disagree that social workers have a duty to protect, however it is when the basis of that intervention in the black family fails to recognize and give credence to the very real strength, richness, and diversity of race and culture that serious mistakes occur in assessment. Generally, there are too frequently devastating consequences for black children and their families. In order to illustrate these issues clearly case studies will be explored as examples of poor practice. I should add that although there are some good examples of social work intervention, these are not representative of the statistics for black children in care, which are disproportionately high when compared to those for white children. This could indicate perhaps, the unequal number of misassessments that are made.

The first case study concerns a referral by a worried neighbour to a team in which I worked. It concerned the care of a black nine-year-old girl. A social worker colleague was sent to investigate an alleged non-accidental injury to the child after the mother was overheard in the garden saying 'get inside the house you my girl, if you don't come in this instance I'm going to beat you'. The social worker went out to visit and it was only by chance on her return that there was a discussion with other members of the team. It transpired that there were no injuries to the child. The mother was very angry about the visit by the social worker, and had said to her

> This is because I used the word 'beat', if I had said 'hit' you would not be knocking at my door. I use it as an expression of frustration at my daughter. My mother and hers before always used the same word. I have had to be subjected to an invasion of my house, and now you say I must make an appointment to take my child to the doctor. You will also be checking her schooling and attendance. This will all go on file too – all for what?

Although the social worker was inclined to take out a place of safety order, other members of the team were able to point out the racial perspectives.

This illustration is, in my opinion, a powerful account of the misinterpretation of language codes. More importantly, it illustrates that when procedures and processes are speedily arrived at, the dangers of misassessment are present. Prior to attending the investigation, the social worker was told by the caller that it was a black family. It could be suggested that rather than consider the racial and cultural possibilities and differences, a Eurocentric view of the information was taken by the social worker, which therefore clouded her appraisal of the situation. This was further exacerbated by the referral form where no distinction of race or culture had been indicated.

Given that information gathering plays a crucial factor in the investigation process, social workers should not fail to consider the wider implications of religion, culture, and language of black families. The Children Act gives credence to this issue which to all intents and purposes may require the use of interpreters to ensure clarification of the issues and in particular extract a more accurate assessment of the feelings and views of the child/young person and family.

Increasingly, social workers are encouraged to liaise with a multitude of voluntary and external agencies such as health visitors, police and schools. These bodies form a useful and close method of evaluating facts and collating information. However, it should be recognized that racism may not be exempt from these agency structures.

Another profound account is illustrated: I was on court duty when a fourteen-year-old Asian boy appeared on a burglary offence. It was his first offence, and one might have expected a degree of leniency given his age, the remorse shown, and the fact that the goods were recovered. However, a school report was submitted to the magistrate which described the individual as 'evil', and coming from an underclass background. The report also contained personal expressions about the high crime rate in the area, all of which bore no relevance to the offence, or the pupil's attributes.

The solicitor representing the pupil asked the court to disregard the report when sentencing – the outcome was a 28-days imprisonment. On release the boy was automatically subjected to a supervision licence, and the black officer allocated the case chose to visit the tutor at school to discuss a work plan. During the conversation, the contents of the report were discussed as the supervisor had not met the young person before, and needed to discount anxieties about the client. The social worker was concerned for his own safety in an office with a young person described as 'evil'. The tutor accounted for the remarks he had casually made, but was eventually able to agree that his report was grossly misleading. The pupil's behaviour amounted to general misdemeanour and, after conveying this to the tutor, he agreed to alter his views and the records on the young person.

This is one of many examples of inter-agency misassessment. It is well accepted that teachers do a thankless job in difficult circumstances. However, they do often have favoured feelings towards one pupil or group above others. This illustration simply demonstrates the complex way in which perceptions are misread and where focus can become blurred. I often wonder, what if this young person had gone to seek help from social workers as a victim of sexual abuse? It is difficult not to imagine that at least initially he may well have been disbelieved, particularly if the investigating social worker had contacted his tutor and chosen to accept the school's assessment. Let us suppose the case had involved a Muslim girl. Are there any differences and would they make any difference to the social worker instructed to complete an assessment?

It could be stated that many teachers find the task of dealing with child abuse stressful and unpleasant. They may lack training in both this vital area and in anti-discriminatory practice at a time of cuts in education and resource shortages. However, schools are a large source of referral to child protection teams. Their contacts have increased substantially in recent years, as a result of child abuse enquiries. Whilst their increased communication of incidents is welcomed, the information supplied must be carefully assessed as the potential for misassessment is extremely high. Schools inevitably base their assessment on different social values and working concepts. The issue of children with special needs is another example of potentially serious miscalculation of abilities and behaviour. Social workers need to obtain accurate accounts for evidence, whilst also protecting individuals and family rights. This makes the task extremely problematic.

The Children Act has strived to ensure that protection is afforded to children, and their accounts are taken on board and are believed. Numerous government booklets and departmental guidelines, including *Working together under the 1989 Children Act* (DoH 1989c), cover this area amply and concisely. I consider that informally, there also exists temptation and pressure for social workers to collude with colleagues in assessment processes. It is obviously useful if all the coordinating agencies are viewing the aspects of abuse similarly. Tension can be caused for the social worker wary about the detrimental effect that collusion could have on black children and families. It is a situation where one agency awaits the others response before supporting a particular factor or rejecting a specific claim.

I would also suggest therefore, that sometimes it can only be a strong social worker who is willing to 'go it alone' and perhaps challenge medical information, police intervention or even their manager's advice. Social workers are reliant upon cooperation at a high level from the police, especially when domestic violence and physical abuse are present. It could be argued from increased research that, as some police officers treat black individuals very differently from their white counterparts, dangers are present. Within the teams I have worked in, a range of experiences are prevalent when social workers speak of their relationships with the police. They often feel suppressed by predominantly male officers who also attempt to play on the gender relationship between themselves and social workers. Black staff experience this to a similar degree, but with the added elements of race and racism.

Black social workers employed in child protection work can be made to feel powerless by the establishment when dealing with child abuse work. Occasionally, but less frequently today, they are expected to be the black 'expert' of the team and carry an all-black caseload. This is both an unwise and professionally dangerous practice for managers and workers to adopt. More importantly it is unhelpful and too cumbersome a responsibility for black staff to take on alone. Within this context, I would support the views of David Divine, Assistant Director, CCETSW. He highlights the fact that the majority of black social workers qualify in predominantly white educational establishments. There is a risk that anti-discriminatory teaching in the curriculum can be ineffective. As a result of internalized racism, some black students, social workers and members of the public may find it difficult to be clear and objective about race issues. Black workers must understand their own limitations of race, culture and religion, particularly in child abuse work.

It is generally accepted that a degree of prejudice exists for us all. A common misunderstanding for social workers, both black and white, is they are exempt from this because of training. I would suggest this to be quite the contrary. Black social workers have to recognize their frequent isolation in teams, and must accept that this position can also apply to service users. Both black and white staff members should be working towards energizing their strengths and capabilities. The use of support groups is important where race issues are concerned, and can ultimately assist in reducing isolation in the management of child abuse work. Community groups and associations can often help in advising social workers on aspects of race, culture, and religion.

HOW TO AVOID MISASSESSMENTS

What is offered here is a broad guideline to the effective assessment of black families. Many of the comments that follow are a result of experience and explain what, in my opinion, a social worker should safeguard against (Okine 1990).

1. Gather all the appropriate information valid only to your investigation.
2. If you have doubts about race, racism, culture and religion, check them out with a more informed party, for example a translator.
3. Consider the use of an interpreter/translator, acknowledging that the user's family members are not generally the appropriate people to consult.
4. Dispel personal myths about black people, in particular negative images of individuals and groups.
5. Keep a clear objective of the reality of the issues, and be prepared to challenge your own prejudices and those of other agents, particularly at case conference stage.
6. Seek out regular, effective supervision and do not hesitate to obtain outside advice for clarity at all times throughout the investigative assessment.
7. Safeguard against others and your own misinterpretation of departmental guidelines and policy; particularly with reference to equal opportunities and 'same race' placement polices for black users.

8. Ensure that referrals are clear, and appropriately distinctive in terms of users' needs and position.
9. Request anti-racist, anti-discriminatory training of the department, or as appropiate, an updated course.
10. Be well prepared at case conference to challenge constructively racist comments and behaviour.

This section relates to report writing on black families where child abuse is a judicial matter.

11. Ensure that court reports and records do not make reference to the country of origin, unless this is relevant. It only serves to portray black people as foreigners.
12. Avoid irrelevant comment on family history/relationships.
13. Avoid commenting on aspects of race, culture and religion without proper information, knowledge, or explanation.
14. Avoid the use of derogatory or patronizing language.
15. Safeguard against describing generation conflict as cultural conflict.
16. Avoid negative, unsupported assumptions which portray black families as being outside the expected norm.
17. Avoid negative assumptions stated as objective fact. This can reinforce stereotypes.
18. Remember that writers' values are manifested by their modes of expression, positive and negative.
19. Resist describing the black child or family in a suspecting manner.
20. Never undervalue or deny a black family's account of experiences of racism.
21. Do not make unqualified reference to school and other agency reports.
22. Avoid providing unconstructive information on a black family's degree of compliance.
23. Indicate in the report restrictions of social service facilities/resources.
24. Resist characterization of black families as unreliable or uncooperative.
25. A gatekeeping (Quality Assurance) scheme should be introduced to vet and monitor anti-racism and discriminatory practice in report writing.

POST-INVESTIGATION ISSUES IN WORKING WITH ABUSING BLACK FAMILIES

The implications for misassessed children and their families can be far-reaching. Many social workers are unaware of the impact of misassessment on the lives of black children and their families when taken into care. Once a black child is in care this is often the beginning of a traumatic experience, during which they are stripped of their identity and exposed to a different cultural experience. Although recognition is given that children should be placed within foster families, some are still placed in residential establishments inappropriately, with institutionalized practices that are racist. Black children can be substantially deprived of their heritage and exposed to abuse of a covert and overt type from staff and other residents. Contact with their natural family may have been terminated, leaving them extremely isolated and vulnerable. These comments are substantiated by the conclusions of my study on 'The needs of black children in care' (Okine 1991). The majority complained about intolerance by staff to diet, skin, hair and health care and the distance from their home communities.

The problems experienced by foster parents in their attempts to be recruited to the list of approved foster carers was another area highlighted. One black foster parent spoke of a three-and-a-half year delay in obtaining approval to join the register, due to checks by the police for criminal convictions. Some white foster parents said they had children placed with them for several months before even having to begin the registration process. This illustrates some of the differences in approach. It is a fact that 'same race' placement policy has existed for some 15 years, but social workers report that insufficient black families apply to foster. I would argue that this is an inaccurate statement. It is the result of institutionally racist policies of local authorities which denies black carers the opportunity of becoming registered foster parents. The above is one example which illustrates how racism operates within social services. They failed to chase the applicants' references from the police, perhaps hoping interest would lapse and the applicant would withdraw. This is an indication of a misassessment of a black foster carer by social workers using white values to assess black families' potential for fostering/adoption.

The recruitment of black foster parents is linked to the social services' inability to recognize that targeting black families necessitates visiting social gatherings and community organizations, and advertizing in magazines specifically targeted to the black community. I would suggest that this is an indication of how black children are misplaced when accommodated by a local authority and their needs insufficiently taken into account throughout the process of assessment. Abused children from black families need black carers.

SUMMARY

Social workers should recognize that the above is not a conclusive list of how to avoid misassessments. It must also be noted that working with black families is an effective, rewarding, stimulating experience when practised within an antiracist framework. Occasionally, calculated risks can be taken. Cross-cultural work is here to stay and social workers have the responsibility to

1. Define the problem.
2. Find solutions.
3. Initiate action.

Black children and their families are no longer prepared to suffer the injustices of misassessment. Comprehensive assessments based on partnership are the key to the future.

CONCLUSION

It is accepted by the author of this contribution that it has not called upon research data to substantiate the arguments. One of the problems with this subject matter is that further research is desperately required, but in a climate of cuts this is unlikely to be a priority for social service departments. I would add that on a personal level, it has been a useful exercise for me to write this account and it is to be hoped that practitioners at all levels will find some of the material relevant to practice and training.

From the information supplied, practitioners in child abuse work with black families need to be clear that assessments should be undertaken within a framework of anti-discriminatory practice. A comprehensive assessment of black families is like all good assessments, complex and time-consuming, and resources are required to meet the needs. There is presently a national decline in the use of emergency protection orders reported by social services. The statistics for disproving a proliferation in the numbers of black children accommodated in care is eagerly awaited. Social workers and managers must be open in their dealings and decision-making with black families if indifference and misassessment of child abuse work is to become a thing of the past. The use of specialized support is greatly encouraged to enhance the quality and verification of cultural and racial shortcomings, particularly in terms of the collation of evidence. If a meaningful partnership of respect is to be achieved the key lies, in my opinion, with the development of a closer, trusting balance of power. If credible work with abusing black families is to be realized social workers must move away from a colour-blind approach, and contribute to a radical review to departmental policy and practice.

C
STRATEGIES

8 Face-to-Face Work with the Abused Child

The phrase 'The Welfare of the Child is paramount' is probably enshrined in every set of child protection guidelines. The Cleveland Report's (1988) statement that a 'child is a person and not an object of concern' has been quoted time and again. The 1989 Children Act specified that we must 'ascertain the wishes and feelings of the child' yet do we *really* care about the abused child? Do we want to help the child who has been abused? Or have we instead created a complex child abuse industry with a myriad of new bureaucratic posts and procedure operators?

An abused child has the right to be the primary client, to be facilitated in a face-to-face way, to make sense of what has happened and, in spite of the trauma, helped to become a survivor. To achieve this, workers will have to be prepared to stay with the child's pain, to experience the confusion and work through the sadness and the anger, in order to encourage healing and foster development.

LISTEN, LOOK, BE AND DO

The actual methods of working directly with children are not complex. What is hard is the self-work which equips us to do it. Four words may help us to begin: *listen, look, be* and *do*.

We have to *listen* – develop a third ear as it were. Maria Colwell told the worker directly 'Don't let me go' and indirectly she said she would like to live on a farm in the country: 'No one would be able to find me there.' Lester Chapman tried to tell how miserable he was by saying he had seen a programme on television 'in which a boy ran away and lived in a tree using matches to keep himself warm.' He said he would like to do that. All the worker did was emphasize the dangers involved. He didn't hear the real message and, because we do not want to bear the pain, we all find it easier not to hear. Sometimes we rationalize this by saying we may damage the child by talking about such painful things. Either way, we leave children locked up in their own misery, turning their hurt against themselves. Sometimes this leads to disturbed behaviour and then we blame the victim. Kimberley Carlile ate her own faeces. She was described as having behavioural difficulties, which was less painful for the worker than facing up to the possibility of child abuse. As the Report says: 'stress can impair our judgement' (Kimberley Carlile 1987).

We have to *look* so that we can see. Theresa drew a fat man with a pole coming out of his stomach. At the end of the pole was the word 'snot'. The teacher reported her to the head who promptly berated her and said 'Don't you dare draw anything like that again!' Three years later aged eleven she became pregnant. The teachers had not seen what Theresa was trying to tell.

We have to *be* the sort of person a child can talk to, taking things at the child's pace, allowing the child to take the lead. This may mean doing an interview in an unorthodox way. One child I worked with would only talk about painful things when he was upside-down doing a handstand against the wall.

Children, if we are relaxed enough, will interview *us* and find out the things they need to know in order to trust us. Percy sat down in a chair and looked at my wall plastered with children's paintings. Skilfully he found out all he wanted to know about me. 'Who drew that one Miss?' 'It's a good painting isn't it?' I said, 'but I don't tell anyone who paints the pictures. Who comes to see me is special between me and that person.' You could see the grey cells working. I kept things confidential. 'Cor! That's a rotten drawing.' 'I think that person tried very hard with his painting,' I said. Grey cells were at work again. I didn't depreciate children. So the interview proceeded until he had found out all that was important to him.

It is very easy to put words into children's mouths when working with them or to move from facilitator to teacher. It needs a great deal of professional discipline to go at the child's pace and to encourage the child to go where he/she wants to and not just to please the worker. This is particularly important when undertaking an investigation when, because we are under pressure, it is so easy to slip into asking leading questions to hasten up the process.

Our last word is *do*. If we are going to 'do' work with children we have to use the child inside us, yet at the same time retain our professional knowledge and judgement. We have to be comfortable with ourselves, as we are. Nothing is more likely to lose the respect, for instance, of a teenager than trying to be 'with it' when we are long past that developmental stage.

Working directly with children can give us numerous headaches. Their feelings of hate, sadness and anger can be overwhelming. The temptation then is to rush in and try to fill the gaps in the child's life. Unless we can be a 24-hour, full-time, continuous, forever-parent, rushing in and playing the role of the good parent will not help. It probably is not what the child wants anyway. What we can offer is warm, friendly, personal help, aimed at enabling them to come to terms with themselves and their actual situation. We may be able to provide new opportunities to build new relationships and mend old ones and to build something out of what was lost. As Doyle (1990) said, 'Abused children are bereaved children. They have lost security, self-esteem and unconditional love.'

THE ISSUES

We have to face a number of issues, thereby helping the child to face them too. It may take us a year of hard work before a parent can meet the child's needs, but the child has to go back to that home tonight. The child's immediate needs may have to be met by outside help and face-to-face work to enable the child to cope with the actual situation.

Sometimes the reason why, as workers, we shy away from direct work with children is that we then discover uncomfortable facts. Direct work with the child may reveal our techniques with the parents are not working. The child may tell us they are still being abused. Looking at things through the eyes of the child may show us our agency is not child-friendly. What we see may even mean challenging some of our dearly held dominant ideas.

Some abused children are very unlikeable. Building on what Crompton said (1980) we have to face the fact that not all adults like children. Not all adults like children at all. Not all workers like children. Not all workers like all the children on their caseload. And furthermore not all workers like all the children on their caseloads all the time. We may not like the abused child but we need to be totally committed to working *with* the child not just *for* the child.

Unfortunately we do not live in a child-centred community. It is crucial that we do not let children down. Whatever the crisis at the office, if we have made an appointment it must be kept. Office politics are not always supportive on this issue. An appointment with a child is seen as low down the list of priorities.

The quintessence of working with children is taking the steam out of powerful issues by sharing. It is showing that we will not be blasted away by the power of the anger or the depth of the sadness. We may have to allow a child to tell us again and again about an event before it can be truly dealt with. After all, we regale again and again every colleague in the office about our four-mile traffic jam coming to work. The only way for an abused child is forwards. We must help them understand and mature through the awful experience. Children can only cope if they are given enough information to make sense of it for themselves inside their own heads – not just by adopting out interpretation of the facts. Yet we must not give so much information that we swamp them and make them paralysed.

The role of a worker is to help children get in touch with the suffering part of themselves: to reassure them that they are understood and respected, so that they can move on, leave the baggage behind and start living for themselves.

WORKING WITH CHILDREN

Before looking at actual techniques for working with children, we do have to recognize that there are some differences from working with adults. But we must not fall into the trap of making the difference bridgeable only by very highly trained experts. There will be a percentage of children who are so disturbed that they need the skills of a child therapist or psychiatrist. However the majority of abused children can get considerable help from a trained social worker or a committed worker in one of the caring professions, provided the worker is supervised and supported.

Age appropriate

The approach used has to be appropriate to the emotional, social and intellectual stage of the child. Time and space may have little meaning to a young child. Rachel had asked when she was going home and had been told by the nurse she was going home on Friday. She kept repeating the same question, as 'next Friday' had no meaning. When eventually her outdoor shoes were put on the bed, she knew she was going home! Young children are concrete in their thinking. Tina watched television. She saw aeroplanes. However when she was told her father was flying to America she became more and more tearful. Finally her mother found out the cause of her intense grief. Her father's arms would get so tired flying to America that he would fall into the sea and get drowned!

Martin, a young friend of mine, was with me when a gushing neighbour asked: 'Do you like going to school?' 'Yes' he replied. I took him to task. 'You hate school.' 'Yes' he replied, 'I like going to school. It's the bit after that I hate!'

Communication

As adults, we tend to use conceptual terms and workers become so used to jargon it becomes part of them. It's very important we find a formula which really explains to a young child what our job is and our tasks are. (Practising with a colleague who role plays a four-year old while another colleague gently squeezes an arm every time we use a word or a concept which is beyond the understanding of the child may help us to discover how good our introductions really are.) Unless we get the beginning right, children can block out everything we say later, fearful as to our true intentions. We have to remember that for the abused child, adults do not have a very good track record.

Children often use their fantasies to tell us something important. It is too easy to get excited and become false. A child might tell us about a man from outer space being caught in a tree. The too eager worker can ruin everything by saying: 'Yes I can see him, he's got red boots ...' The child knows it is a fantasy and we can't see it. Such a comment proves ourselves liars and pretty insensitive ones as the spaceman wears black boots anyway!

Workers and courts are having to become more sensitive about the fact that children don't tell painful stories in a logical way. They may tell bits of the story or may test the water first by saying that Uncle Tom sexually abused them to see if we are prepared to believe and can bear the awfulness of what could have happened. The trouble is that Uncle Tom was in Singapore at the time. Before the child feels prepared to tell the true story the adult world has made the child out to be a liar. The adult and child world is not the same.

The misunderstandings go both ways. Adults often start a conversation with children in such stereotyped ways. 'Hello Johnny, how old are you?' 'What do you like best in school?' Would we approach Mr Brown like that? We may have to play quietly alongside the child until the child makes the first movements towards us. Perhaps the adult can open the subject by talking to themselves in an almost lullaby voice. Communication is a reciprocal giving and receiving of thoughts and feelings. The worker's body posture and tone of voice must convey empathy and understanding. Being on the floor with the child means you can respond on so many planes. Remaining seated on a chair is so limiting.

A child may begin to feel valued when the worker feeds back something he/she said several weeks ago. In ordinary life parents cannot listen for 24 hours a day to everything a child says. But this is precisely the gift of a worker – an hour of 100 per cent attentive respectful listening. Here is an adult who *wants* to know how the child feels and what the child's real wishes are. As workers we must watch the fact that children become experts in assessing what adults want, and say things just to please them.

The aim is to get children to be able to share their feelings and, once they are expressed, to be in control of them so they are not destroyed by their anger and sadness. It may be that the feeling has to be validated and they need to be told that they have every right to feel angry – they shouldn't have been subjected to the event. The art is to help the child get the feeling out in a helpful way. One boy client of mine said it was like being all tied up in a big plastic bag. The feelings couldn't get out so they just came and attacked you. Once we had jointly broken out of the bag the feeling just floated away into the air getting weaker and weaker.

Communication can be silence. Silence can be healing. One of my clients came in to 'report'. He was eleven. After a formal report on school and home he then lapsed into silence. I tried everything to build communication between us. Finally I gave up and week by week he regularly came and we went through the same ritual. When the next group of students came to the student unit I decided I was making such a mess of the case it should be referred to a student. A few days later I met the mother in a market. She went on and on and never stopped talking. She complained Mark was furious with me for transferring him. At last I heard the message. He appreciated our joint supportive silences. Here I was trying to help a student to get him to talk which was the last thing that was going to meet his needs.

Children may also of course keep workers at arm's length by keeping up a constant superficial prattle so that they do not get near to painful subjects. Children can fool us by appearing bright and cheerful but it is a facade. On the other hand children may keep silent because they are afraid the information or the feelings may destroy you too. Telling about the sexual abuse the first time broke up the family, so they had better keep quiet this time. Alternatively, silence may mean the child is so depressed nothing will make things any better so there is no use trying.

Words

Words means different things to different people. 'I'm here to help you' may have a very hollow sound if the word 'help' has always been used as a prelude to a beating. Words can also have different significance if English is not the child's first language. In different parts of this country 'starved' can mean hungry or cold. Butterflies were my downfall. A rather hostile boy client admitted to being interested in butterflies. At last I thought, a breakthrough. I read up on butterflies and eagerly awaited John's arrival. I began to talk about butterflies. He patiently let me go on, although his face became perplexed. 'Butterflies?' I said. Getting desperate, I said: 'You know, butterflies, insects with wings.' A ray of amusement. Butterflies was the nickname given to tractors in his neck of the woods! The fact I could laugh at myself and make a mistake *did* make the breakthrough. The adults in his life were obsessional people like his stepfather who never made mistakes. Adults were not all the same, he concluded after the butterfly incident.

Third objects
Children since the dawn of time have used third objects to communicate: before it is safe to respond to your parents you try it out on your teddy bear. So we too must use third objects with children. They do not have to be expensive products. To explain about being removed you can use a paper clip, a paper hankie, a coin, to represent the main characters.

Face-to-face work does not have to be done in special 'suites'. Some of my best work has taken place sitting on the stairs in a block of flats. However, if you do have a separate private room where there will not be interruptions it can be a great help. It is often useful to have special stickers that the child can put on the door to show that for the next hour that is his or her private space. Another sticker can make it clear that the person accompanying the child will be waiting there until the end of the session. If a child is frightened of being abandoned, the person's most favourite possession, like a handbag or jacket, can remain in the room with the child as a link object.

As self-esteem is so important with abused children, a special box with the child's name on it can be kept with some of the regularly used third objects. This can be in the room ready and waiting for the arrival of the child. A range of toys can be in the room but not so many as to be a distraction: paper, pens, dollhouses, plasticine or hand puppets are all useful media.

Rules
If the child is going to be having several sessions it should be made clear how many are being offered. Some rules will have to be established. The first will be about confidentiality. In simple terms, it has to be honestly faced that the worker is part of a team who will want to know how the child is progressing. In addition, the child is part of a family, and everyone must be

kept informed. At the end of each session, time is put aside to decide how the child and the worker will feed back to the parents the main thrust of the session without going into every detail. Equally, the parents and worker must share with the child the main issues that they discussed in their session. This process can be a useful way of passing positive messages. 'Last week John knew you were cross because of his behaviour. We have been trying to see how John can find better ways of handling things.' The message back from the parents' session might be: 'We have been working with your parents on why they got so cross with each other and then we are trying to see how we can make things more relaxed at home.'

Other rules may be that the toys in the room have to stay there, that the worker may have to ensure no serious damage is done to people or property and that time limits will also be strictly adhered to.

SOME EXERCISES

Judging by what people say on my courses, the main problem for many of them seems to be how to start. The suggested third-object exercises which follow are divided into three groups: (i) starters, (ii) working with issues, and (iii) finding self, although some could be used at any stage. The exercises must be adapted for the particular child and often the child will take the lead and change them further to meet his or her special needs.

Starters (to break the ice)

Faces
Either the worker or the child draws first a happy face, just a circle with eyes, nose and smiling mouth. The child is then invited to draw or write all the things that make them happy. This phase should not go on too long. It is usually the worker who wants to stay in the happy mode. Then the child is asked to draw a sad face: 'What things make you sad?' This often opens the doors to some of the abusive things that have been happening to the child. But, as in all interviewing, it is following up the tone of voice – the sudden change of subject, the

body language and helping the child to share – which is important.

Mailbox
Children often find it hard to introduce a subject they want to talk about. A box covered in bright wrapping paper with a slot at the top and a door at the side is a useful ploy. The child and worker draw or write the topic they want to talk about and it is put in the box. Then the folded bits of paper are pulled out one by one and become the subject of the next session (Redgrave 1987).

Storm
The worker or child draws an island: 'Who would you like to come with you on the island?' The order often tells you a great deal. 'Then it's discovered there's a volcano so a ship comes to rescue you. Who goes on the ship first, second, etc?' The skill is keeping everything open and not suggesting who should be allowed to come. It is usually the worker who has problems about who is left to be swallowed up by the volcanic ash! This game tells the worker a great deal about the child's feelings towards significant people in his or her life.

Card game
For older children special packs of cards can be made out of blank postcards bought from a stationers. Some of these will be left empty but on most of the cards will be an unfinished sentence such as, 'I feel mad when ...' 'I feel glad when ...' 'I feel sad when ...' The sentences can be made to fit the individual child. The pack is then dealt, preferably by the child, to the child and the worker. As each card is turned to the side with the legend on it the person has to finish the sentence. The worker has to be prepared to be honest and to convey professional messages to the child. 'I feel sad when children are unhappy.' 'I feel glad when a child can share how he or she feels with me.' The children will also be sending significant messages to the worker.

Me cards
A big sheet of card is drawn up with twelve sections. The child and the worker put words and drawings into each section. The rule is that nice and nasty things that have happened to the

child are put alternatively into each square. A dice is thrown and a counter used to count along the board. Where the counter finishes up, that is the subject to be talked about.

Working with issues (These exercises are aimed to help talk about the abusive incident)

Sociograms
You could not ask a child to draw a sociogram. However, if you start with a big sheet of paper and ask children to draw anywhere on the sheet a circle to represent themselves, you are beginning to create this construct. You then suggest they draw a circle for a person who is at home. They can put it anywhere on the sheet, near or far from their own circle. So the game progresses. It is interesting to note the size of each circle and where they put circles representing different family members and who they leave out. A great deal can be learned from this exercise, always checking back with the child that you have got things right.

House
Draw a symbolic house or flat with a front door. Walk hand in hand with the child to the drawing pinned to the wall. 'What would I see, Tommy, if I opened the door? Who would be in this room? What would they be doing?' This exercise is a safe way of talking about people who live with the child and what happens at home from his or her point of view.

Boxes
A large number of cardboard boxes are required for this game and are a way of getting out angry feelings. A child is asked to draw or write on a box what makes him or her most angry: then on the next box, and so on, until we have a pyramid. Then, and the worker must enter energetically into this game, the child must shout out what he/she hates and punch the top box to the floor. Then shout out the next legend and the next. The worker must encourage vigorous shouting. The game is even better if after each box has been written on it is stuffed with newspapers as fast as the child and worker can go. The newspaper makes the box more resilient to kicking and therefore far more satisfying. The stuffing of newspapers is also satisfying and gets rid of a lot of anger.

Fears
Newspaper is a marvellous medium. It is cheap. Paper is cut into interesting shapes. The shapes can represent either fears the child has or people the child hates. The child can jump on the shapes or throw screwed up balls of newspaper at the shape pinned to the wall. Again this game will not work unless the worker joins in and encourages a strong display of feeling, reassuring that this is a safe way to get rid of negative responses.

Special friend (for the younger child)
The worker chooses a toy which he or she feels comfortable with and which always remains in the worker's car when not in use. Children will check this out – sometimes years later. If it is not there, we have been proved unreliable. This toy is a special friend and is used to talk to children. Children will talk to teddy – whisper in his ear about things they would not tell the worker direct.

Finding self (These exercises can be used to help children build up their self-esteem)

Spider's web
Two boxes are kept under the worker's desk. One contains treasures such as buttons, bottle-tops and coloured paper shapes. The second contains pieces of coloured string. In the centre of the sheet is a drawing of the child. The child sticks the various 'treasures' on to the sheet of paper to represent the people in the child's life. Time is spent talking about each person. The string goes from the self-portrait to each person symbolized on the card. Different coloured string will probably represent the child's different feelings towards each person. When finished the Picasso-like production can be sprayed with silver or gold aerosol and taken home as *me*. The important thing is the validating conversation throughout the exercise.

Shields
Explain that in the olden days people had shields. On the shields were emblazoned paintings that represented the particular warrior. A shield is created for the child. A cardboard shape is divided into sections and in each quadrant the child draws something positive about themselves.

Hands
On a large piece of paper the worker draws round the child's hands. On one hand the child writes all the things he or she likes doing, saying, and places they like going to. On the other hand are written all the things he or she does not like doing, saying, or going to.

Champion cup
A board is divided into several squares and the child draws what he or she is good at and finally awards himself or herself the specially drawn challenge cup which the worker and the child have created.

Dressing up
The advantage of dressing up and playing various roles allows the child to experiment with roles they do not usually play – like being a person everyone fêtes, being famous or being admired.

CONCLUSION

It is difficult to describe each exercise fully as they really need to be demonstrated, but the important thing is that each child adapts the games to his or her own needs. The exercises themselves are simple. It is the skill and sensitivity of their operation that counts, helping the child to confront the abuse and to find ways of working through the experience to become as whole a person as possible.

Fortunately, children will forgive many false starts and will assist in finding ways of helping. But Mary Edwards's experience should always be a salutary reminder:

> I longed to talk to my social worker but always the barriers came down as soon as I sat at the desk; that invisible barrier that had been systematically constructed during the previous visits. I would sit in silence, inwardly pleading for her to ask me about my feelings. I would become angry. I felt she ought to have known how I was feeling especially because of her position and if she did not know then she was avoiding the issue and she didn't want to waste time. I wasn't important enough.

9 Legal Strategies

*Caroline Ball**

The law has a significant part to play in child protection and the provisions of the Children Act 1989 have been described by Lord Mackay as 'the most comprehensive and far reaching reform of child law which has come before Parliament in living memory'. The Act was drafted with the intention of securing a better balance between the rights of children to have their voice heard, the rights of parents to bring up their children without interference, and the duty of the state to intervene where a child's welfare requires it. The compexity of the human situations for which the legislators must provide the legal parameters of decision-making means that getting the balance right is one of the most difficult tasks that they face. For the past 40 years attempts have been made to achieve this balance by means of piecemeal measures to correct perceived swings too far in one or other direction, which often subsequently proved to be over-corrections (Rowe 1989). Only practice experience and research evidence will demonstrate whether or not the Children Act 1989 succeeds where other less comprehensive attempts have failed.

---

*Caroline Ball is Lecturer in Social Work Law at the University of East Anglia and editor of *The Magistrate*.

BACKGROUND TO THE NEW LEGISLATION

By the 1980s the need for root and branch reform of both the substance of child care law, and the court structure within which it was administered, was only too apparent to social work and legal practitioners trying to make sense of complex and confusing provisions. Even worse, there was abundant evidence that parents and children felt peculiarly disadvantaged when caught up in an incomprehensible system they felt ill-informed about and powerless to challenge (House of Commons 1984, Cleveland Report 1988).

The origins and progress of the legislation through the consultation and parliamentary process have been addressed elsewhere (Ball 1990, Eekelaar and Dingwall 1990), and are beyond the scope of this chapter. What is important is to consider the issues that informed the content of the new provisions in which both public and professional opinion played their part. Had the law provided adequate means of protecting children from abuse, criticism of the statutory framework might have been more muted. As it was a number of highly publicized reports on inquiries into the deaths of children, either in care or very well known to social services departments, showed that the then existing legal framework for child protection was both lacking in important respects, and so complex that it was both inadequately understood by practitioners and at the same time open to widely discrepant interpretation (Beckford 1985 and Carlile 1987, Cleveland Report 1988).

At the same time research evidence published during the mid 1980s demonstrated in a variety of ways the damaging effects of the poor child care practice which flourished within legal provisions which allowed, or even encouraged, resort to statutory orders rather than co-operation with parents (DHSS 1985). The daunting legal disadvantage of parents when trying to challenge local authorities' decisions – particularly over contact with their children in care – resulted in some of those children being quite literally 'lost in care' (Millham et al 1986), and, as was particularly apparent in Cleveland, the voices of the children being too often ignored when they should have been listened to (Cleveland Report 1988).

CONCEPTS, PRINCIPLES AND DEFINITIONS

Implemented in October 1991, the Children Act 1989 comprises a comprehensive and coherent package of provisions operating within a set of clearly expressed principles, with the magistrates' family proceedings court, the county court and the High Court having concurrent jurisdiction to deal with family proceedings (Figure 9.1). It replaced not only the confusing, overlapping, much amended provisions of the many statutes concerned with the so-called public law, but also the private law provisions regarding the care, maintenance and upbringing of children, previously enacted in separate legislation.

In order to place the child protection provisions contained in Parts IV and V within the context of the whole Act it is helpful to understand the way in which they are informed by, and must be interpreted in the light of, the concepts, principles and definitions which apply to all other family proceedings, and in particular how they link in with local authorities' powers and duties under Part III. As the Lord Chancellor frequently reiterated throughout the passage of the Bill through Parliament, although each of its twelve parts relates to different aspects of child law it must be read as a whole: the 'whole' meaning not only the Act, but also the mass of accompanying court rules, regulations and guidance which make the provisions workable. As a foundation to practice in implementing the Act and to inform interpretation of the delegated legislation and guidance the Department of Health has published a very helpful guide, compiled by a working group of child-care academics and practitioners, under the chair of Jane Rowe (DoH 1989b).

The Act introduced the concept of 'parental responsibility' to underline the shift away from parents' rights in relation to their children, and to allow greater emphasis to be placed on the continuing reality of parenthood, regardless of the breakdown of adults' relationships with each other (DoH 1989a), or the need of the local authority to intervene to provide care for the child. The ways in which parental responsibility may be acquired are set out in detail in Part I of the Act. An understanding of the implications of the distribution of parental responsibility is now central to child-care work.

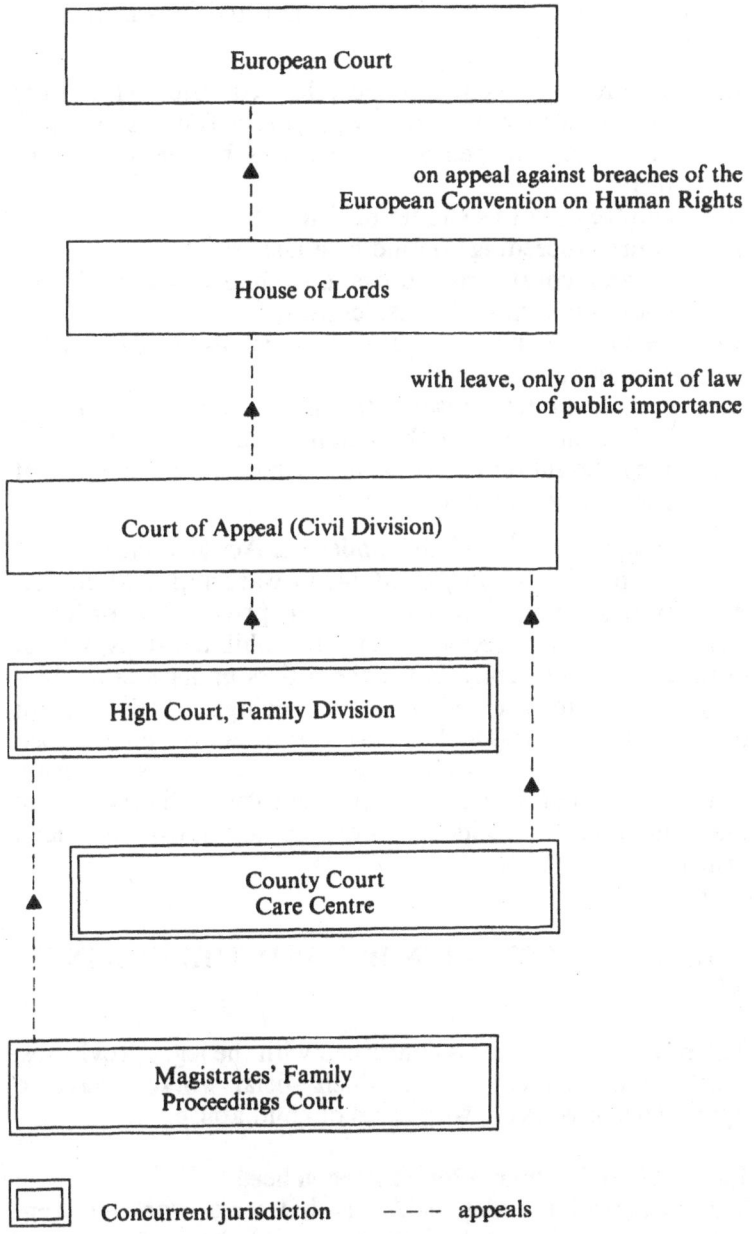

Figure 9.1 *Courts with jurisdiction in family proceedings*

The principles that underpin all the provisions in the Act are that:

(i) children are generally best looked after within the family, with both parents playing a full part in their upbringing, helped when necessary by the local authority;
(ii) children's voices should be listened to;
(iii) court proceedings should be a last resort;
(iv) in any court proceedings the child's welfare is the court's paramount consideration;
(v) delay by courts in reaching decisions is likely to be damaging to the child;
(vi) courts should consider the whole range of available orders and not only those applied for; and that
(vii) they should only make orders which are likely to be of positive benefit to the child.

The range of orders available under the Act give the courts a flexibility previously only available in wardship proceedings. A marked feature of this is that the private law orders – residence, contact, specific issues and prohibited steps, set out in section 8, and family assistance orders under section 16 – may be made in care and other proceedings, whether or not they are applied for (DoH 1991a). For instance a court considering a local authority application for a care or supervision order may, if that is what they consider to be in the child's best interests, make a residence order to a relative or friend instead.

CHILD PROTECTION WORK AND THE CHILDREN ACT

The rest of this chapter is concerned with the legal provisions, checks and balances within which social workers have to operate when working with cases of child abuse.

Local authority services for children in need

The presumption under the Act is that social work intervention, when needed, will wherever possible be in the form of supportive services to children and their families on a partnership basis. Part III can be seen as the cornerstone of the Act so far as child-care work is concerned and this applies as much to children in need of protection as to other categories of children in need. Section 17 replaces the negative provisions in the Child Care Act 1980 s1 with a positive duty to:

> safeguard and promote the welfare of children within their area who are in need; and so far is consistent with that duty promote the upbringing of such children by their families, by providing a range and level of services appropriate to those children's needs.

A child 'in need' is defined under s17(10) as one who is unlikely 'to achieve or maintain, or to have the opportunity of achieving or maintaining, a reasonable standard of health or development without the provision to him of services by a local authority ...'; or his health or development is likely to be significantly impaired, or further impaired, without the provision of such services; or he is disabled. 'Development' means physical, intellectual, emotional, social or behavioural development, and 'health' means physical or mental health s17(11)).

As well as a duty to children in need of protection from abuse, local authorities also have preventive and investigative duties under the Act which relate to all children. These include the duty to 'take reasonable steps' through the provision of services detailed in Schedule 2, Part I, 'to prevent children within their area suffering ill-treatment or neglect' (para 4), and to 'take reasonable steps' designed to reduce the need to bring care, criminal or other family proceedings relating to them.

The whole range of services which local authorities must or may provide in order to carry out their preventive role are also set out in Part III and schedule 2 part I (DoH 1991b). This includes a duty to provide accommodation for any child in need within their area who appears to them to require it. The provision of accommodation, which replaces reception into care under the Child Care Act 1980 s2, is a voluntary arrangement, and anyone with parental responsibility may remove the child from accommodation at any time (s20(8)). The forward-looking grounds for obtaining emergency protection orders (see p.148) provide a means, if agreement cannot be reached, of securing a child if precipitate removal would be likely to cause significant harm.

The duty to investigate

Local authorities may be put under a duty to make investigations into a child's circumstances either when the making of an emergency protection order, or the placing of a child in police protection, alerts them of the need to do so. This duty also arises when a local authority is provided with information which gives 'reasonable grounds to suspect that a child who lives, or is found, in their area is suffering or is likely to suffer significant harm' (s47). The investigations have to be undertaken to enable the authority to decide whether they should take any action 'to safeguard or promote the child's welfare' (s 37) (DoH 1991a).

In order to carry out these duties the authority has to take all reasonable steps to ensure that access to the child is obtained. Refusal of access or information about the child's whereabouts constitutes grounds for obtaining an emergency protection order, and a duty to do so 'unless they are satisfied that his welfare can be satisfactorily safeguarded' in some other way. Similarly refusal to co-operate with an assessment of 'the state of the child's health or development or of the way in which he has been treated' in order to determine 'whether or not the child is suffering, or is likely to suffer, significant harm' may lead to an application for a child assessment order under s43.

Court-ordered investigations

Under previous legislation a court could make care or supervision orders on its own initiative, or on application by a local authority, in 'exceptional circumstances' in the interests of the child's welfare, in various proceedings in which decisions regarding children were being made. This effectively provided a 'back door' into care without the need to establish statutory grounds, and was strongly criticized by the Law Commission for this reason (Law Commission 1987). Under the 1989 Act care and supervision orders can only be made on the application of the local authority (or an authorized person) on the basis of satisfaction of the threshold conditions set out in s31. Where a court becomes sufficiently concerned about children, who are the subject of any other family proceedings, to consider the need for care or supervision they may order the local authority to investigate the child's circumstances (s37) and consider whether to apply for a care or supervision order, provide services or assistance for the child or the family, or take any other action. When a court orders an investigation under s37, provided there is reasonable cause to believe that the threshold conditions in s31 are satisfied (s38), it may at the same time make an interim care or supervision order. The local authority must report back within eight weeks and inform the court of any action they propose to take, or give reasons for a decision to take no action.

Compulsory intervention
The shift towards the use of voluntary arrangements rather than compulsory intervention is at the heart of the Children Act; there will however always be cases in which compulsory measures will be required, and others in which the possible use of compulsion may encourage co-operation previously lacking, without eventual recourse to court. Previous legislation concerning local authorities' duties to investigate situations in which children appeared to be in need of protection contained an implicit presumption in favour of compulsory measures; under the Children Act the duty to investigate is strengthened and extended but the choice of route chosen to safeguard the child's welfare is left more open.

Courts are helped to focus on the issues they must take into account when reaching decisions regarding children's welfare by the 'welfare checklist' in s1(3) which requires the court to have regard 'in particular to:

(a) the ascertainable wishes and feelings of the child concerned (considered in the light of his age and understanding);
(b) his physical, educational and emotional needs;
(c) the likely effect on him of any change in his circumstances;
(d) his age, sex, background and any characteristics of his which the court considers relevant;
(e) any harm which he has suffered or is at risk of suffering;
(f) how capable each of his parents, and any other person in relation to whom the court considers the question to be relevant, is of meeting his needs;
(g) the range of powers available to the court under this Act in the proceedings in question.'

To help maintain the focus on the child's welfare, in most

public law proceedings a guardian *ad litem* (GAL), an independent social worker appointed by the court, will be appointed for the child at an early stage. The role of the GAL, which is considerably extended under the Act, is as far as is possible to ascertain the child's wishes and feelings, instruct the child's solicitor, advise the court on: parties, the timetable for the proceedings, the making of interim orders, including possible discharge of an emergency protection order, and to prepare a report for the court. Where the child and the GAL disagree over the child's needs, a child of sufficient age and understanding may give his own instructions to his solicitor, and the GAL will represent her own views to the court, with legal representation where necessary.

Child protection in an emergency
The immediate protection of children in an emergency requires wide powers available without delay, either to ensure that a child is removed from a situation of danger, or remains in one of safety when threatened with removal. Preventing abuse of such powers requires that they shall only be exercisable in circumstances in which immediate protection for the child cannot be secured in any other way, and be open to challenge at the earliest opportunity. The contrasting dissatisfactions with place of safety orders under the Children and Young Persons Act 1969 informed the provisions in Part V of the Children Act (Allen 1990, Ball 1989, Cleveland Report 1988, Henry 1987). The extent to which the former broadly framed provisions allowed discrepant and sometimes abusive practice explains the detail contained in Part V, which leaves little margin for discretionary interpretation.

Emergency protection orders
The EPO is intended for use only in real emergencies: anyone may apply to a court or, with leave of the justices' clerk, to a single justice who is member of the family proceedings panel, ex parte (without anyone who might oppose the application either being present or being served notice) for an order, on the grounds that

> there is reasonable cause to believe that the child is likely to suffer significant harm if ... he is not removed to accommodation

provided by or on behalf of the applicant; or ... he does not remain in the place in which he is then being accommodated

or where enquiries are being made by a local authority, anyone authorized by them, or by the NSPCC, and they are denied access to the child (s 44).

An EPO may be made for up to eight days and the child or anyone with parental responsibility may apply to a court for discharge of the order after 72 hours, provided they were not served notice and were not present when the order was made. An EPO may be extended once for up to seven days if the court has reasonable cause to believe that the child will suffer significant harm if it is not extended. During the period that an EPO is in force the local authority will have limited parental responsibility and will therefore be able to make day-to-day decisions in regard to the child, whilst parents retain their parental responsibility subject to the EPO. There is a presumption of reasonable contact between parents and child; however the court may lay down requirements regarding contact which shall or shall not take place, and regarding more than routine medical treatment or investigation – which a child old enough to decide may refuse.

Police powers to protect children

Police protection
Under s46 where a constable has reasonable cause to believe that a child would otherwise be likely to suffer significant harm he may remove the child to suitable accommodation or take reasonable steps to ensure that he remains where he is. The section sets out in great detail the steps that must be taken by the constable to ensure that parents, the local authority and the designated police officer responsible for inquiring into the case are informed, and that the child's wishes and feelings are considered. Police protection may only last for up to 72 hours; however during that time the designated officer may apply for an emergency protection order under s44. If granted this will begin with the first day on which the child was taken into police protection.

Police warrants
Where it is either apparent at the time of the application for an

EPO, or subsequently, that anyone attempting to exercise powers under the order is being, or is likely to be, denied entry to premises or access to the child, a court or single justice may issue a warrant authorizing a police constable to exercise those powers, using force if necessary (s48(9)).

Entry of premises to save life and limb
The Police and Criminal Evidence Act 1984 (s17(1)) restates the common law power of the police to enter and search any premises for the purposes of 'saving life or limb'. Where appropriate, exercise of this power could be followed by reception of the child into police protection.

Child assessment order
This is a new order which had no parallel in previous legislation. It may be applied for only in court, on notice, by a local authority or the NSPCC (as 'authorized person') on the grounds that there is reasonable cause to believe that the child is suffering or is likely to suffer significant harm; that an assessment of the child's health and development are necessary; and that it is unlikely that a satisfactory assessment will be made in the absence of an order. If the court hearing the application believes that an EPO is justified then it should make one instead of the order applied for. Guidance suggests that CAOs will only be appropriate in cases in which 'a decisive step to obtain an assessment is needed. . . . and informal arrangements to have such an assessment carried out have failed' (DoH 1991a Vol I para 4.8).

Recovery order
Where a child in care or the subject of an emergency protection order or in police protection has been removed or has run away from care, or is kept away from any person who has care of them as a result of that order, the court may issue a recovery order under s50. The order operates as a direction to produce the child, and authorizes their removal by any authorized person, and the entry and search of specified premises by a police constable.

Care proceedings
Proceedings under s31 and most other applications for public law orders are commenced in a magistrates' court, unless they

result from an investigation ordered under s37 in which case they are heard by the court ordering the investigation. Cases commenced in the magistrates' court may be transferred, either laterally to another family proceedings court able to hear the application more quickly, or, on the basis of agreed criteria, to the local county court care centre. Exceptionally cases will be referred on from the care centre to the Family Division of the High Court. Figure 9.1 on p 143 shows the court and appeal structure for family proceedings.

The only means whereby a local authority can assume parental responsibility in regard to a child under the age of seventeen, or sixteen if married (other than for the very short term of remand or an EPO), is by means of a care order made by a court, on the basis that the threshold conditions are satisfied, and that the order is likely to contribute positively to the child's welfare (s1(5)).

Under s31(2):

> A court may only make a care order or a supervision order if it is satisfied –
> (a) that the child concerned is suffering, or is likely to suffer, significant harm; and
> (b) that the harm, or likelihood of harm, is attributable to –
>   (i) the care given to the child, or likely to be given to him if the order were not made, not being what it would be reasonable to expect a parent to give him; or
>   (ii) the child's being beyond parental control.

Under the Act 'harm' is defined as ill-treatment or the impairment of health or development (further defined in s31(9)); and whether harm suffered is significant depends on comparison with 'that which could reasonably be expected of a similar child'. It would seem inevitable that in due course a body of case law will refine these definitions.

Prior to a final hearing an interim care order or supervision order, or any private law orders under s8 of the Act, may be made on the basis that there are reasonable grounds to believe that the threshold conditions exist. The presumption that delay is harmful, and the provision within the court rules for directions hearings and the establishment of timetables for proceedings, means that any interim order beyond the first, which may be for up to eight weeks, will have to be well justified.

Court rules provide for directions hearings, the setting of timetables for the proceedings and the exchange of witness statements and reports in advance of the final hearing. Courts, including the magistrates' family proceedings courts, have to give reasons for their decisions, and all parties have a right of appeal (see Figure 9.1 on p 143). Although the proceedings are single stage civil proceedings courts have to be satisfied that the threshold criteria set out in s31(2) are satisfied before they decide which, if any, order to make. The orders available are:

- a care order;
- a supervision order to the local authority or in certain circumstances to a probation officer. The order may include directions to the child; a residence requirement; impose requirements on a person responsible for the child (with consent); or require the child to attend for medical examinations, or, if the relevant conditions are met, to undergo psychiatric or medical treatment. Supervision orders cease to have effect after one year unless extended by a court up to a maximum of three years (s35 and Schedule 3 Parts I and II);
- any s8 order;
- a family assistance order under s16.

The effect of a care order, which lasts until the child is 18, unless discharged, is to give the local authority parental responsibility for the child together with the parents, who retain the right to exercise any aspects of their parental responsibility which is not in conflict with local authority decisions in respect of the child's upbringing. Regulations regarding the placements of all children 'looked after' by the local authority, which includes those in accommodation as well as in care, are detailed and elaborated on in Volume 3 of the Department of Health's Guidance and Regulations. Contested issues of contact with a child who is the subject of a care order are dealt with under s34 which allows parents and others much greater powers to challenge local authority decisions regarding contact than in previous legislation.

CONCLUSION

The fact that the substantive law under the Children Act not only has the previously lacking merits of clarity and consistency, but is also administered in a system in which the courts have concurrent jurisdiction, and work to almost identical rules, is a substantial step forward. Whether or not the law now provides, as so many hope it does, the legal framework within which good child-care practice can flourish and social workers can achieve the delicate and (history would suggest) elusive balance referred to in the introduction to this chapter will only become apparent over time.

10 Child Protection Skills

Government ministers and inquiry reports have recently laid great stress on the special skills required to work with abusing families. It would be a mistake to see these as separate and distinct from those required to work with other groups of clients. However, experience has shown that there are skills that do need to be sharpened and used with particular sensitivity and authority when working in the field of child protection. As this is such an important issue, it is worth pulling together under one heading the various references to skills that have been made previously in this book, thereby providing an inventory of the skills required by any worker seeking to be effective in child protection work.

THE SKILL TO PERSEVERE

Time and again child abuse situations have become dangerous when the case has been allowed to drift. Workers need persistence and the skill of keeping going. The Malcolm Page Report (1981) stated that this means 'simply not taking no for an answer', constantly probing one's assumptions, testing whether they are based on adequate and reliable data and checking on 'the correct implementation of procedures' (Karen Spencer Report 1978). Because of all the subjective feeling around, it is easy to get blown off course. Good practice is about checking and checking again. Persistence is particularly called for where initial visits fail to gain access. As in the Richard Clark (Clark 1975) case, even if an appointment is not kept with another agency, the matter still has to be meticulously checked out and followed through. Monitoring is often equated with passivity. Monitoring *should* mean doggedly checking out, constantly reviewing. Acceptance does not mean we lose our critical faculties.

SKILLS IN CONFRONTATION AND THE USE OF AUTHORITY

Confrontation is not the same as being aggressive. Confrontation can be therapeutic. At the centre of confrontation is the possibility of change. Workers in the field of child protection must have the belief that authority can be used constructively. In the famous phrase used by Blom-Cooper in the Beckford Report (Child in Trust 1985), authority is an 'essential ingredient in any work designed to protect abused children'. There are, of course, negative aspects of authority, but child protection workers need to develop the therapeutic aspects. Clients who abuse need to feel that workers can set boundaries: boundaries that help contain the destructive forces within the parents; boundaries that won't allow the parents to destroy themselves or the child. Workers need to be authoritative and confident if they are not to be destroyed by the destructive aspects of the abuser or washed away by the obscene feelings of some perpetrators.

Because abusers feel empty and lack self-esteem they will cheat and lie. Workers therefore have to develop the skill of challenging them in a warm and caring way, having the ability to adopt a healthy scepticism without rejecting the client. The chance of success comes from confronting the behaviour without attacking the person. Social workers have often been accused of pussyfooting around in the name of the principle of acceptance. Corby's study (1987) noted that abusing parents 'preferred social workers to be more open about their child protective functions'. Corby concluded from his survey that 'there should be no equivocation about the social control role ie social workers do need to come to terms with their responsibilities and duties *vis-à-vis* children considered at risk.' Not to do so, as Jordan (1976) rightly says, 'infantilises the parents'. Not confronting means that 'rather than helping, the social worker can instead become part of the client's nightmare. The situation is never defined; the reason for supervision is never spelt out, the problem is never brought out into the open'. Workers need to be up-front about what needs to change and within what time limits. This also means that workers have to be crystal clear themselves. To be woolly and evasive only makes clients deep down angry and is the best way to achieve 'drift'.

Confrontation is a vital tool especially in handling sex abusers. Cognitive distortions have to be challenged. Because sex offenders manipulate, rationalize and minimalize, workers have to be authoritative about what has to be worked on and faced.

THE SKILL OF CREATING ACTION

Child protection work can grind workers down. Supervision must encourage the skills of innovation, adaptability and flexibility. Team leaders need to look at office routines. Do they infantilize workers? Does the office atmosphere encourage apathy and futility? Does the team give each member real support to 'get up and do'? Or is the office style so 'laid back' that all action is considered beyond the pale? Is the group a team really working together? Are staff meetings interesting and revitalizing? Is it expected that staff will discuss cases that they are finding difficult in a challenging but warm empathetic way, thinking up new approaches and ways of responding? Or are staff meetings boring, administrative affairs, that everyone tries to avoid?

SKILLS OF ASSERTIVENESS AND BEING APPROPRIATELY SELF-CONFIDENT

To be able to offer a child protection, workers need to be secure in their social work knowledge. At the very least, workers need to know about the needs of individuals at each stage of human growth and development. They need to know about child-care and a range of social work approaches, and avoid jumping on the bandwagon of the latest craze. The method must be adapted to each client. Workers must also know the law and be confident in their knowledge of the duties

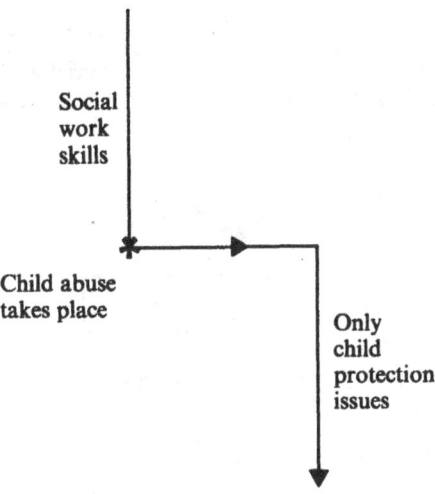

Figure 10.1

and responsibilities delegated to them by the law and their agency. It can be reassuring for some abusing parents if the workers are clear and firm about what their job is. To 'waffle around' creates the sort of insecurity that can actually increase aggression.

Unfortunately some workers see the law as something negative instead of an available therapeutic tool. Taking legal action is seen as the last resort, to be used if all else fails. Certainly legal action is often seen as a social work failure. This is where the Integration of Law and Social Work (ILSW) approach is so valuable, as referred to on p 27. It is very easy to get trapped. Workers visit a family using all their social work skills. Then abuse occurs and the worker abandons the social work approach and homes in on child protection issues alone. This leaves the family feeling betrayed and confused (see Figure 10.1) by the change of direction.

Instead, in any case where there is the faintest possibility of child abuse, the worker needs to draw on social work techniques and draw from the law and marry the two into one. It will be an uncomfortable marriage but a live and vital one (see Figure 10.2). The worker's responsibility, made clear in the

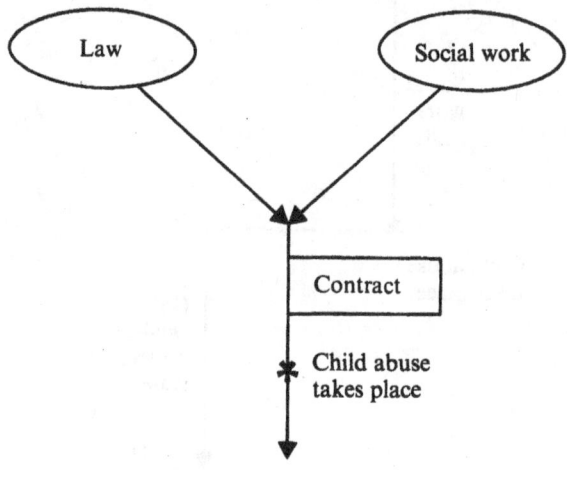

Figure 10.2

original contract, means legal action, if necessary, is part of a holistic approach.

In exercising authority, workers are integrating the care of social work with the control of the law. Many abusing parents too have to bring the two – care and control – together if they are to become 'good-enough' parents as this is what so much of parenting is about. So many see the two elements as separate from one another.

Abusing parents need the experience of firm but non-retaliatory authority. Many clients in their past lives were unable to challenge in a safe way, because they feared either that they would be destroyed if they did, or that the fragile family system would be destroyed if they confronted it. This new experience enables confrontation without destructuion. Workers must show that they will not disintegrate but can hold their position. This is reassuring to the adult client.

Games can be played with us to try to stop us operating our legal responsibilities. These are numerous. See p 27. 'I've got so many problems I'm a special case, so I'm above the law.' 'You say you care – but if you really cared you wouldn't punish me by taking me to court.' 'Why are you taking me to court now, when you didn't before?' The parents can make us feel professional failures: 'If you had helped me more we wouldn't be in the position now of having to take legal action.'

The ILSW approach faces the reality of the situation but as well as finding out who did what to whom and how and when, is aiming to give an understanding of the total situation. A skilfully handled court action should lead to greater understanding and all those involved beginning to work out improved responses to the reality of what has happened. In all this social workers have to keep a fine balance between their responsibility towards the client and their responsibility towards society and the law.

Workers need to work with themselves about having the authority of the law, if they work for social services or the NSPCC. Other agencies have to be clear as to what authority they have and their duty to refer to the statutory authorities. Workers have to watch feelings that emerge from childhood about being 'sneaks': feelings about authority that have more to do with our own battles with our own parents.

THE SKILL OF WORKING WITH HOSTILITY

Child protection workers have to be courageous. This emerges from the mixture of perseverance and confrontation. If a household is too dangerous for a worker to visit accompanied by a colleague then the question has to be asked: 'Is it safe for the child to remain?' Certainly if workers are going to undertake child protection work they must not have a powerful need to be liked. We have to be able to work with clients who hate us. The most valuable tribute is when the client turns round and says, 'I did it all myself, you were no use!'

Parents have every right to be hostile. Who likes to be investigated? We have to hang on to the fact that progress can be made with people who resent and continually attack us. A positive relationship is not the only one that makes progress. We may need to hold, contain and set boundaries with the violent husband or co-habitee. To duck this responsibility is to make the child vulnerable. The violent client will not make progress unless someone can set the boundaries. He or she is frightened of the powerful forces within them and terrified by their own violence. The worker must not therefore be afraid. This is easier said than done. I am not suggesting workers put their own lives at risk. Training, with the sensible support of colleagues – which may have to be the police – can begin the process. If the client can frighten off the worker then he will feel no-one can cope with his aggression. He is powerless and a victim of his own violence.

SKILL IN WORKING IN AN INTERDISCIPLINARY TEAM

Child protection workers have to have a good look at themselves. There are some workers who are natural loners. You cannot go it alone in child protection work. No one worker can take the emotional onslaught. We need the services of many agencies. We may need conflicting styles of work with the same family. For instance, one worker may need to be authoritatively setting boundaries so that the other worker can be empathetic and accepting. If we are part of an interdisciplinary team no one worker can see themselves as the only one who understands. Sibling rivalry has to be addressed. Each agency has to be seen in context. The interdisciplinary approach is not a spongy mish-mash. Each worker in the team has to be clear about their individual role and discover how the conflict of perspectives can be used constructively. It is also essential to be clear how and what is to be communicated between workers and family and by whom. We need to watch that the interdisciplinary team is a team and not a pyramid of pecking orders with the paediatrician at the top and the family aide at the bottom.

SKILL IN WORKING WITHIN TIME LIMITS

Some workers can achieve a great deal if given a considerable amount of time. However, in child protection work, time is often not available. The child, if we hang around too long, will be dead. Team leaders and workers therefore need to be clear about what tasks have to be achieved within definite timescales. Supervisors need to be constantly looking at how time is used. Burnt-out workers can waste a great deal of time chatting on the phone and making innumerable cups of coffee. This only increases the general feeling of tension! Offices must be able to offer flexibility so that tasks that have to be undertaken within a definite time limit can become top priority because other work will be taken on by a colleague. Of course if the whole team is burnt out and under strength, then cases may drift and mistakes may be made. This is so often the criticism when tragedies occur.

SKILL IN WORKING IN STRESSFUL SITUATIONS

Child abuse work is stressful. Social work courses must address this issue and include teaching on how workers need to pace themselves. Teaching on burnout should be part of basic training, as should teaching students how to relax. Be firm with yourself and take a complete break at lunchtime however short, since eating a sandwich and making a telephone call at the same time is the fastest way to burnout. Burnt-out workers make mistakes and put children at risk.

Agencies need a pastoral service for staff or money to pay for outside consultancy. Using such a service must not be seen as a sign of weakness but as a strength, a strong sign that the issue has been recognized and the worker is tackling it.

SKILL IN PROTECTING THE CHILD

Some workers who have been trained to work with the family as a whole find it difficult truly to keep in mind that the child *is* the paramount client. Anne Elton (1988) put it very well when she emphasized 'that the child is and remains our primary client, not the family; if their interests are in conflict then we have to consider the former as paramount.' Child protection workers have to be comfortable with this philosophy and acknowledge from time to time that protecting the child may mean damaging the family. Some families are dangerous and children have a right to be protected. We may be able to work in partnership with most parents, but some may have been so traumatized themselves they are lethal to their children and cannot form a postive partnership with workers. To shut our eyes to this small group is not child protection.

Abusing families need all the skills we can muster but the above nine skills are at the core of child protection work.

11 Child Protection Conferences

The British solve their problems in the personal services by setting up committees. When the issue was problem families co-ordinating committees were set up. When the issue was child abuse in 1974 case conferences were recommended. In 1991 case conferences were renamed child protection conferences in the government guidelines issued that year.

Conferences have thus become one of the most important tools in the management of child protection cases, but they should not be the stars of the whole show. They are only one of the stages in the whole process. They are neither an end in themselves nor a talisman that will ensure the final outcome will be beneficial to the abused child, nor are they an easy option. Participants and chairpersons have a professional responsibility to work hard to understand the possible interactions that can prevent objective outcomes and to struggle to secure the best possible interests of the child. Otherwise child protection conferences can become dangerous.

The 1991 guidelines *Working together under the 1989 Children Act* have crashed together various concepts into a working process (DoH 1991c).

First there are the philosophies of the 1989 Children Act which stress the importance of involving parents and children in any decision-making process and insist that the welfare of the child must always be the paramount concern. The Act also provides the statutory framework for child protection and the guidance constantly reminds the professionals of this.

Secondly, although governments have stressed the importance of working together, the 1991 guidance has put the matter more categorically and unequivocally so we must work on a 'multidisciplinary basis with a shared mutual understanding of aims, objectives and of what is good practice'.

Thirdly, this process must always take account of gender, race, culture and disability.

Each of these elements should be an integral part of all child protection work but they are particularly evident in the child protection conference, which is called after investigation under s47 of the Children Act.

AIMS AND PURPOSE

Conferences, whether they are initial or review, aim to bring the family and professionals together to share information and concerns and to make plans. If the conference decides to place the child's name on the Child Protection Register, a named keyworker must be appointed and a core group of closely involved professionals identified. A child protection plan should also be drawn up.

Keyworker
Even where another professional has more face-to-face contact with the family, the keyworker must be a representative of the agencies with statutory powers, ie the social services or the NSPCC. The keyworker is the lead worker, providing focus for communication, co-ordination and interagency contributions to the assessment, planning and reviewing of the case.

Parents and children
Several years ago I nailed my colours to the mast and stated that parents should attend child protection conferences (Moore 1986). I was therefore particularly pleased with the stance of the 1991 guidelines. Previous government guidance was somewhat equivocal on the subject but the 1991 guidance is emphatic that parents (and children where appropriate) should attend part, if not the whole, of the conference in all but the most 'exceptional circumstances'. Where the Chair does decide to exclude a parent or where parents are reluctant to attend a conference, a method of presenting their views to

the meeting must be found. Similarly, if a child is too young, or is unwilling to come to the conference, ways of putting the child's views must be devised, whether by making a tape, helping the child to write a letter or ensuring that someone has been fully briefed to give those views.

Attendance at a conference is an intimidating experience for anyone who is not used to it and particularly for the parent or child, who find themselves the focus of attention. They need help in preparation and the opportunity to bring a friend or supporter, and attention should be given to their needs when fixing the time and place. If there is conflict and disagreement within the family, it may be necessary to arrange for separate attendance. If the conflict is between the child's and the parent's needs, the child's welfare must take precedence. All this requires skilled chairing in addition to careful preparation and it should constantly be made clear that a conference is neither a tribunal nor a court and is not making a decision about the guilt of an adult but the protection of the child. The detailed arrangements for the attendance of parents and children are a matter for local Area Child Protection Committee (ACPC) agreement: the principle is that they should be included and their views made clear. This is not an easy option and is often an uncomfortable one for the professionals involved, who may have to struggle to keep the welfare of the child as their paramount concern when faced with the needs of the parents.

The guidelines have widened their view of 'parents' to include caring adults and the word 'family' is now used. This could mean several members of the wider network. All of this has implications for the size and length of the meetings. Some guidance on these issues will be required from individual ACPCs.

THE CONFERENCE ITSELF

The cauldron beneath the surface
Child protection conferences are very complex forums. In fact they can become a veritable cauldron. Each member of the conference arrives bringing with them a trail of feelings, preconceptions, values and fears. These may include anger that the adult client has let them down, guilt that they themselves did not do more or take throwaway lines more seriously, fear

that a carefully built reputation could now be destroyed, jealousy that another agency could possibly disrupt a successful treatment plan, or even despair that nothing can be done with the family anyway!

Denial
Perhaps the most dangerous attitude is denial: denial that anything very serious happened anyway. 'He just touched her – nothing more.' Dingwall et al's (1983) researches confirm that professional workers tend to choose the 'least stigmatizing interpretation of the child's condition and least coercive form of intervention possible'. The trouble is that it is easier for the worker to identify with the pain of the adult than the pain of the child. We see in the mirror our own suffering as children and try to ward it off with myths, elusions and dominant ideas.

Stereotypes
It is against this background that we stereotype. A certain amount of stereotyping is essential in our everyday lives. It would be too much of a shock to the system to relate uniquely and freshly to every individual, but stereotyping can become highly charged with emotions, particularly in times of stress. We hide behind the defences of stereotyping so we can feel safe in the positions we hold. We call attention to all the facts that support our view and divert from all that contradicts our stance. So all health visitors are. . . . All police are. . . .

Different perspectives
The trouble is we are all attracted for very different reasons to the jobs we do. A colleague once described it as each of us having a different centre of gravity. We then get trained into our profession, take on the values and philosophies of that profession and we take on board the basic concepts and assumptions which form the frame of reference which we use as the set to solve the problems within our own purview. The tools and methods are self-evident to us but not to other disciplines. The trouble is not, as it were, at the centre of each professional concern but where the disciplines overlap. Unless we belong to a particular religious group there is no argument that we want the surgeon to be the professional who operates. We are equally certain of what problems we would take to the

hospital social worker. The trouble starts where the two responsibilities meet. The social worker wants time to help the wife come to terms with the fact that her husband will only have one leg and demands that the patient stays for an additional three weeks in hospital. The surgeon wants the bed for his next operation as quickly as possible.

It is always a mistake at conferences to try to achieve a false consensus. Chairs need to feel secure enough to tease out differences and to act occasionally as devil's advocate if the group has agreed too quickly without looking at all the alternatives. Carefully managed, the family could benefit from conflicting responses. We need to pull together all the different perspectives to get the full picture. All participants need to be alive to the different priorities and pace of work for each discipline. The teacher has a group of children. Caring for one child must not cripple the learning potential of the majority. The social worker is focused on the needs of the individual child and child protection may be, for the NSPCC worker, the main aim of his or her agency. Health visitors often have case loads in the hundreds, with tasks that span the whole child population for the area. The time that can be spent with one family is necessarily limited. It is not easy to weld together disciplines into an interdisciplinary team.

Power games
Unless some of these issues are acknowledged and accepted, power games can take over. Old historical feuds can continue. Pecking orders can be established. I have personal memories of attending a conference with a student. She presented her report in which she commented that she thought the mother got uptight just before her periods and was therefore at risk of assaulting her child. There was studied boredom in the room. But when the paediatrician mentioned he though his research in pre-menstrual tension was relevant to the case, everyone leaned forward in respectful concentration. Of more serious outcome was what happened in the Beckford case (1985). Blom-Cooper comments coyly: 'We hesitate to conclude that the reason for such dismissal of Miss Knowles' information was the inferior status accorded to the health visitor by the doctor.' Olive Stevenson adds, 'One has only to observe the difficulty many women have in breaking into formal conversation, even in relation to strength of voice, to see how unhelp-

ful the interaction of gender with occupation may be' (Stevenson 1988).

Pecking orders
Pecking orders are inevitably influenced by who attends the conference. The nursery nurse in charge of the child's room does not attend. Her opinion is sought by the officer in charge, who does. The problem is that the officer in charge cannot answer the supplementary questions from personal experience. The nursery nurse feels treated as a second-class citizen. She has the information but is not given the status of an invitation to the conference. The same is true for teachers. It is the class teacher who should attend but there are logistic problems. The school may have different teachers for different subjects. The school cannot be denuded. A compromise may have to be found. The officer in charge takes over the children's group. The class teacher attends and the headteacher takes over the class. Obviously there will have to be some delegation of responsibility and trust that the worker will not exceed his or her remit and in this the child protection conference may have to have some tolerance if it is going to get the best possible information.

Dynamics
Chairs particularly have to use their knowledge of small groups to understand what can happen at a child protection conference. After all, what could be more complicated than a small group of people looking at another small group – the family? As has been stated earlier, child protection conferences can re-create amongst themselves the original abusing family and the conflicts between agency workers may be rooted in the original family dynamics rather than in the issues at the conference. Forces noted many years ago by Hoffmann (1965) can take over: 'Groups tend to produce unanimous decisions and discussions tend to increase the uniformity of their members' individual judgements.' His final pay-off line is significant: 'There is no guarantee that unanimity produces truth.' Often Chairs falsely believe consensus at the conference means the meeting is right. It is often the lone quiet voice crying in the wilderness that has to be listened to earnestly.

Conflicts

When a child protection conference is stuck and going aimlessly round and round in circles it is wise for everyone to see what is really happening is that the case has stimulated a deep-rooted conflict of philosophical or cultural positions. What might be the issue is the battle between parental rights and children's rights. But the battle becomes even more convoluted if the belief is that we can always find middle ground. This may be impossible just because of the powerlessness of the child. The issue may be around attitudes to residential care, some believing in the myth that all residential care is bad and others fired by a need to rescue the child at all costs. The conflict may be even deeper. What may be promoting the battle on the surface is very different perceptions of family life. As Stevenson (1989) states: 'We all need to scrutinize our own "individual, cultural and class assumptions" about what is good and bad in family life in order to determine what ... can be jettisoned as non-essential and what is ... central to a child's physical, social and emotional health.' Living in a multi-cultural society some of our assumptions will be constantly challenged. Because a child rearing pattern is different it is not necessarily bad.

Another battle that can rumble along and suddenly burst into a conference discussion is the long and continuing conflict between therapy and court action. The two are not mutually exclusive. Court action can be a therapeutic process if handled skilfully. Unfortunately it is so often seen as therapy *or* court action. This raises the issue of the attendance of representatives of the legal department at child protection conferences. Legal advice is always valuable but the lawyers should be on tap and not on top. A child protection conference is not a court of law. The decision for the social services department to take legal proceedings should, I suggest, rest with the director of social services' representative, obviously taking into account legal advice. It may be in the interests of the child to get a legal decision on matters where the evidence is unsure. Though departments cannot be foolhardy over financial affairs, cost should not be the deciding factor. The best and the most appropriately specialized advocates must be employed. The role of the legal department of the local authority is so wide they cannot always be specialists in child protection.

Two heads are better than one

We are told two heads are better than one so a number of heads should be even better: not so. According to the original research by Stoner (1961), groups make riskier decisions than individuals. Pruitt (1971) and recent research suggests that groups move towards a riskier direction or a more cautious direction. Certainly I have seen conferences where, after taking a very risky decision, the conference gets stuck on another problem where they become excessively cautious. These outcomes probably spring from several causes. If the anxiety can be shared or diffused then the reduced anxiety felt by each individual will allow them to make a riskier decision. The adage 'familiarity breeds contempt' can also operate. Because people are so familiar with the material they can become blasé. This is why 'one shot players' are so useful at child protection conferences. A colleague who seldom attends can see things freshly and starkly. Perhaps too they can demand services because they will not reappear for some time. If a worker has to be aware that he/she may require a favourable consideration in another case next week he/she may be afraid to challenge too hard for fear of losing a comfortable professional relationship. The charisma of one of the members or the chairperson may skew a conference and lead to a decision being taken which is more risky or less risky than the individual would take on their own initiative. Kane (1975) and Brearley (1982) make the point that: 'The more eager an individual is to belong to a group the more he will conform to its norms.' This process can start in the waiting room when those attending either deliberately or unconsciously make it clear they know each other. So there is an 'in' and an 'out' group. This is sometimes ambivalently acted out by those who regard themselves on the outside: 'Everything has been fixed by the social services before the meeting.' However this group is often grateful to leave all their responsibility to the social service department. Perhaps the report by the social worker, written in the belief it saves time, should not have recommendations in it at the first stage of the conference. Recommendations should be submitted later at the meeting. However if the social workers do not, as they so often say, want to feel everything is dumped on them by the other disciplines, they should look at their own attitudes. They have, alongside the police and NSPCC, statutory powers. They may be the key-workers, but an interdisciplinary approach is essential. No one department or worker can carry a child abuse case. Particularly as so often the family is in need of so many services provided by a variety of agencies. Though social services have a major role to play the professional responsibilities must be shared and other agencies made to feel a crucial and integral part of the process.

Rule of optimism

Conferences can become totally skewed. A very anxious worker can get empathetic colleagues focusing on them and the awful experience that they are having and turn the attention away from the welfare of the child. The rule of optimism or suspended disbelief can mean risks are ignored. In *Spycatcher* Peter Wright describes how the continuing rule of optimism meant the moles in MI5 could go on operating even when there were clear pointers as to who they were (Douglas 1989). Optimism is more comfortable than painful truths that require legal action.

CONFERENCE MEMBERS

A conference is as good as those who attend. It is also as good as the quality of the contributions made. Those who do not attend can also influence what happens.

Absentees

GPs take a lot of stick for their absences. Perhaps we idealize the amount of information an inner city doctor in a group practice has about families. The GP may believe he hasn't much to offer. But there may be subtler reasons for his absence which are not cured by payment for attendance. What is a good time for other professionals and parents cuts right across surgery and clinic times. Doctors are trained to wield considerable power and make life and death decisions. They are trained to *do* things. The usual time for a consulation is about ten minutes. An hour-and-a-half case discussion is not the doctor's arena. In his/her arena the doctor takes the lead. At child protection conferences the Chair is occupied by a social worker.

Another absentee at many child protection conferences is

often the lack of information and knowledge about the father. Unless the male client is on probation or a member of the armed services and therefore has his own worker, he is often not included in the programme of work. Because some agencies in inner cities are not encouraging staff to visit late at night owing to the high rate of mugging on some estates, the father who works can be forgotten. Boyfriends can themselves try to avoid attention by insisting they have no legal status towards the children. A man who visits a family regularly where there are children must have a powerful influence and must therefore be evaluated as part of the family dynamics.

Agencies that have responsibilities towards the adult members of the family must never forget the child protection conference is focused on the child. Probation officers for instance must not see themselves as speaking up or advocating on behalf of *their* client. The child is the client at the conference. Attendance of parents at conferences may help to get the balance right.

Another group that can get lost at conferences is the children who have not been abused. They can be as badly damaged as the index child and may need as much help. Siblings of the sexually abused may feel guilty they didn't know their brother or sister was being victimized. Worse, they may feel devastated that they suspected but felt powerless.

Agencies can be absentees too and have to be actively sought out and encouraged to attend. One of the responsibilities of the Chair may be to spot gaps in the information provided. It is a human temptation to fill the gap with conjecture which after a few meetings is taken as actual fact.

Saboteurs and the antidotes

The dominator   There are people whose behaviour can sabotage a child protection conference. There is Mr/Ms Dominator who can take over the meeting. The Chair has to value the often good contributions of this character but make the point that others must have their say. It is sometimes helpful to state that it is a well-known fact that the quietest person at the meeting often has the most valuable piece of information.

The whisperer   Then there is Mr/Ms Whisperer who can be so distracting. You can neither hear what is being said in the main meeting or the private conversation! The Chair has to smile and firmly but gently ask that 'Could all comments be shared otherwise it breaks up the meeting and things are missed.'

The joker A sense of humour is always necessary, but a funny joker can take a meeting right off into a blind alley just as the group is beginning to get down to the important issues. This is probably why he/she went into action in the first place. The Chair needs with a straight face to thank the joker. It may be necessary to acknowledge it was a good joke but to state: 'I think you have taken us unhelpfully off course.'

'I've got a client' This character is brilliant at red herrings and always has a case he/she wants to talk about. The Chair has quite firmly, and before this individual has taken a second breath, to state: 'We must get back to *this* case.'

Mr/Ms Timid The skill of the Chair must come to the fore with this attender. They often do have crucial information. Large groups are not their scene. They often present badly. The difficulty is that often the information is tainted by its presentation. The Chairs must value publicly the contribution of Mr/Ms Timid, perhaps asking questions they can answer to encourage the flow of their contributions.

The groupie There are people who evade their responsibilities, perhaps even the boredom of their jobs by filling their diaries with conferences. No one can then say they are not working. They particularly swell the ranks where there is a salacious case being discussed. Having as a ritual at the beginning of the conference to ask the attenders to state their purpose in being at the conference sometimes helps. The added push may also be constructive. When they state they haven't got any contributions to make, the Chair can courteously state to the conference that the groupie is obviously frightfully busy and therefore the conference will excuse them. You of course have to know your groupie and be sure they have nothing useful to contribute or take back to their agenices.

The silent ones The silent majority can be a real danger. If every worker is accompanied by a team leader and manager then there can be more people making decisions about a family who do not know the family than do. In addition feelings about the worker rather than the facts about the family may become more influential.

Other problems

Time Another saboteur of conferences is time. Humans can only concentrate for quite a short period of time. Unless carefully paced by the Chair too much time is spent on pooling information and not enough space is left for analysis and seeking and developing alternatives. All the recent enquiries have emphasized the danger of 'drift'. Planning is therefore most important. Child protection plans may literally be vital and must be plans that can work with the actual resources available. Everyone must be absolutely clear as to who does what, with whom and when.

Jargon Jargon can abort communication. Jargon can be a valuable form of shorthand between fellow members of the same discipline. However games can be woven around jargon. Its use can signify you are a member of the inner group, privy to the latest research, member of an elite working party. Jargon can create a mystique around the simplest of subjects. The anecdotal story of the 'grommits' is a good illustration. The doctor mentioned the child had grommits inserted in her ears at a conference. Everyone said 'Oh yes' and nodded knowingly. Later an observer asked who knew what grommits were. Only the health visitor knew. The significance was missed because no one would admit they didn't know. The trouble is that so often jargon can become so much part of our vocabulary that we don't know we are using it. It blocks communication and creates barriers, sometimes even anger.

THE DARKER SIDE

In a group the more irrational and darker side of our nature can collude and create racism, sexism, heterosexism, homophobia, classism, ageism and disabilityism. The trouble is that the comments are not made in a direct manner. The prejudices and fears come wrapped up in so much verbiage. Often comments are not made, just implied by a throwaway line or a gesture. All participants at child protection conferences have to be alert to their own and other irrationalities. Stripped of the words the irrationalities look the ridiculous statements that they are and do not show how dangerous and hurtful they are. Irrationalities are dangerous because they affect the responses and plans we make. To make the point I have listed a few just by way of illustration but in no way am I suggesting that the list is exclusive.

Racism
- Because white workers are afraid of being perceived as racist they may not investigate a case of child abuse in a black family thoroughly enough, so the black child is not protected.
- A member of the conference makes the half statement: 'It's a black family' implying that being black equals being a problem.
- A black child who is abused may be placed in double jeopardy if he/she is placed in an institution where all the staff are white. The child has no black model *and* has been removed from his/her family. To add to the problem if the centre does not offer the relevant skin and hair care the black child truly suffers from institutional racism.
- The worker implies that the family is at fault for not having English as their first language, instead of acknowledging it is the agency who is to blame for not providing translators and brochures in the right language. Many more agencies should pay for staff to go to classes so that they can speak fluently the tongue of the largest ethnic group in their area as interpreters can block an interview if they don't understand the social work process.
- Implication is made that sexual and physical abuse is a natural part of the family culture of a particular race group: 'Sexual abuse all takes place in Asian families.' 'Afro Caribbeans beat their children.' 'So we don't need to do anything.' You only have to look at the statistics for sexual and physical abuse in white Anglo-Saxon families to see what a lie all these are.
- There is a false belief that black mothers are 'endlessly

resourceful, able to cope in great adversity, essentially unsinkable' (Tyra Henry Report 1987). Thus the black mother is left in intolerable situations.
- Conversely racism may miss the strengths of black families.
- Not providing the appropriate services for ethnic groups is racist and must be recognized as such.

Sexism and gender issues
- The implied statement is made that the children are the mother's responsibility. Fathers are allowed to feel they don't have to play a role *vis-à-vis* the children.
- There is the false belief that if sexual abuse takes place it is because the wife hasn't given the husband sufficient sex. The wife is thus blamed.
- Similarly there is the false belief that men can't be expected to control their sexual urges. The wife is ill so it's understandable if he sexually abuses the child!
- There is the false belief that women don't sexually abuse children.
- There is the false belief that it is gays who sexually abuse children.
- There is the insidious throwaway line that by being sexually mature the girl 'asked' to be sexually abused.
- There is the suggestion that if a male is sexually abused he will inevitably become a homosexual.
- There is the false belief that lone mothers are inevitably a problem.
- There is the false belief that all plump, large-bosomed women are motherly; tall, thin, small-bosomed women are not motherly; and only women can mother anyway.
- There is the false belief that only two heterosexuals can appropriately bring up children.

Classism
- There is the false belief that all sexual abusers are old tatty men in raincoats; that articulate, well-educated middle-class people don't sexually abuse.
- There is the false belief that the working classes are of low IQ and are inarticulate.
- There is the false belief that the best way to solve a

problem is to call a meeting (a process so beloved of middle-class professionals).
- There is the false belief that if you are poor it must in some way be your own fault.
- There is the false belief that the poor are so accustomed to poverty that they can be expected to get by in conditions which no middle-class family would be expected to tolerate (Tyra Henry Report 1987).
- There is the false belief that child abuse, especially sexual abuse, doesn't occur in the upper classes.
- There is the erroneous belief that sexual abuse has always gone on in boarding schools, so why bother!
- There is the false belief that social work professionals do not abuse.
- There is the false belief that it's OK to send children to public schools but it's wrong to put children into care.

Ageism
- There is the false belief that all grandparents are benign and good. Grandmothers wouldn't sexually abuse!
- There is the false belief that if an adolescent boy sexually abuses it's just the growing-up process and he doesn't need help.
- There is the false belief that only the latest research is valid.
- There is the false belief that if you are middle-aged you've learnt a lot from your experience; young social workers can't be qualified, experienced and wise. Wisdom only goes with age!
- There is the unwillingness to face the fact that young sexually abused children can sexually abuse in residential, day care and child-minding situations.
- There is the false belief that young babysitters don't sexually abuse.

Disabilityism (Marchant 1991)
- There is the false belief people wouldn't abuse disabled children when in fact some sexual abusers find the vulnerability and powerlessness of disabled children particularly appealing.
- There is the false belief that children with disabilities are

easily led and that the rate of false allegations will be particularly high.
- There is the false belief disabled children don't feel so it's OK to sexually abuse them. It isn't harmful because they can't distinguish between sexual touching and touching which is part of routine care.
- There is the false belief that if disabled children have been abused it's better to leave well alone and not upset them further; they can't express their feelings anyway.
- There is the false belief that trying to prevent abuse of disabled children is too complex and upsetting so it's better not to try.
- There is the false belief that as so many people are involved with the care of disabled children the authorities would know anyway.

Stripped of the surrounding words and innuendo all these dangerous beliefs look ridiculous and not believable. However at the child protection conference if we are not supervigilant they can powerfully skew our whole meeting.

CHAIRPERSON

Competent chairing of such complex forums as child protection conferences is vital if the process is not to become a dangerous one. As the guidelines state: 'The skills of the Chair are crucial.' Some areas have made chairing a full-time activity in order to facilitate the building-up of the necessary expertise and to minimize delays. The Chair has to be a member of the social services or the NSPCC where this is the local agreement. The Chair should be trained for the purpose and in my view should be given time and space to continually update professional knowledge about child protection. Managers who have been or will be involved in making decisions about the case should not chair, so that there is an objective view. The focus of the conference must always be the child as the primary client and must transcend the interests of parents and carers if there is conflict. The Chair is responsible for the ethos of the conference including ensuring that the focus is on the child and everyone is clear about other members. Though the Chair may not personally carry out the task, he/she is responsible for ensuring the appropriate people are invited. An agreed place and time ensures the maximum attendance, particularly of those people who are working with the family. Waiting facilities must be adequate. The duties of the Chair must also include the managing of the inevitable cups of tea so that it doesn't disrupt the whole meeting and people may be unable to hear as teacups are rattled and whisperings echo about the receiving of biscuits! The room should be the appropriate size, airy and warm.

All child protection conferences should have someone who is trained to take notes and to produce minutes of the meeting. The format and circulation of the minutes should be pre-agreed. The 1991 guidelines are absolutely clear: 'The conference Chair should never take the notes.' The notes should be quickly despatched. It is not possible to cover all matters about child protection conferences here. It would be good advice to say before attending your first conference read *Working together under the 1989 Children Act* (DoH 1991c) from cover to cover and also study the latest copies of your local ACPC guidelines. Then from time to time re-read; bad practice has an awful habit of insidiously creeping up on one!

Epilogue

It is fitting to end this book with the same message of Mary Edwards which was quoted in *The ABC of Child Abuse Work*.

'If only the professionals had done their job effectively I, like thousands of others, might have been spared such a lot of unnecessary emotional traumas . . . .'

Appendix

WHAT IS THE CAUSE FOR CONCERN – WHO DID WHAT TO WHOM – AND HOW AND WHEN?

Social biographies
(For each parent or cohabitee)

Parent/cohabitee
Name. Alias. Date of birth. Age.
1 What are the good experiences?
2 What are the bad experiences? eg deaths, separations, hospitalizations, abandonment.
3 Was the parent brought up by harsh discipline?
4 Medical history (physical, psychiatric). Possible intelligence; emotional history; previous significant relationships?
5 How does the parent cope with stress or conflict situations?
6 Evidence of rigid/obsessive personality?
7 What is the state of the partnership? Is there any nurture in the partnership?
8 Is there evidence of excessive dependence needs?
9 Are there 'ghosts' around, eg powerful/destructive/supportive grandparents, parents-in-law, wider networks?
10 Previous abuse of this or other children.

Child Name. Date of birth. Age.
1. Early history: good/bad experiences; bonding; premature?
2. What stage is the child at?
3. Has the child been abused? Recently? In the past?
4. Disabilities: physical/mental?
5. Was the child difficult to rear? Aggressive? Passive? Withdrawn?
6. Is the child scapegoated?
7. Current and past health: medical/psychological/emotional? Possible IQ?
8. Development: motor skills, language, height, weight, toilet-training?
9. School: Approach? Achievements? Learning problems? Speech difficulties? Friendships/networks?
10. Physical appearance and presentation?
11. Was the child wanted? Right sex? Did the child disrupt the partnership?
12. Is the child now provocative/hyperactive/rejected/ignored?
13. What sort of discipline is used?
14. How does the child fit in with the rest of the siblings?
15. How does the child see things? Comfortable in race and gender?

Other siblings
1. How have siblings been affected by abuse?
2. Significant information?
3. Is work required with siblings?

Child-rearing skills
1. Do the parents understand and respond to the child's needs? Understand milestones?
2. How do parents perceive parenting? Too high/low expectations?
3. Do they get any joy from the children?
4. What are the trigger factors? What causes most frustration?

Effects on the child
1. Has the child been abused? What is the effect?
2. Has the child been interviewed alone? Feelings worked

with? What does the child feel? What is his/her understanding of the events?
3. Where is the child now?
4. Where is the child in the bureaucratic process? Have there been delays? Adjournments? Court hearings?

Family interaction
1. Is there eye contact; physical contact and touching?
2. Do family members talk to each other? How?
3. Contact with the child: is it loving/cold, rough?
4. Does the family protect the child?
5. Do the family do things together? Are they bonded in hate or love? Dyads/alliances?
6. Would the drawing of a critical path of events or sociograms be of value? If so, do it.
7. Power structure: is there submission in the family?
8. Family strengths as well as weaknesses?
9. Family system.

Physical conditions
1. What is the structural and physical state of the home? Rent? Debts?
2. Finances? Financial commitments? Is there long-term poverty?
3. Has there been a recent change in finances? Geographical location? New members of the family eg boyfriend? girlfriend?
4. Employment of members of the family?

Precipitating event
1. Has there been a recent precipitating event? Actual or perceived by those involved?
2. Worker's viewpoint?

Family network
1. Is the family isolated?
2. With whom is there contact: relatives/friends?
3. Which professionals and para-professionals have contact?
4. Is the neighbourhood supportive or hostile?

Response to help
1. What has been the experience of other helpers? What work has been attempted?
2. What information is already available? Date of information. Is it stale?
3. What works/does not work with this family?
4. What resources are actually available to help?
5. What resources are missing/need to be created/substitutes found?
6. Any themes emerging from past professional contacts?

How does the family see its problems?
  This is most important of all!

Legal action
1. What legal or administrative action has been taken?
2. What legal or administrative action is proposed?
3. Previous court appearances and outcomes?

Child protection plans
1. Detailed child protection plans. Face-to-face work to be attempted with the child.
2. Proposed work with parents, family or significant others?
3. Short- and long-term aims and objectives.
4. Success criteria.

References

Abel, G. G., Beck, J. V., Mittleman, M., Cunningham-Rathner, J., Rouleau, J. L. and Murphy, W. D. (1987), 'Self reported sex crimes of nonincarcerated paraphilacs', *Journal of Interpersonal Violence*, 2.3.25.
Allen, N. (1990), *Making sense of the Children Act*, London: Longman.
Ball, C. (1989), 'The current and future context of emergency protection', *Adoption and Fostering*, 13, (2), 38–42.
Ball, C. (1990), 'Children Act 1989, origins and expectations', in *Social Work and Social Welfare Yearbook No. 2*, Milton Keynes: Open University Press.
Barnett, Sharon, Corder, Francesca and Jehu, Derek (1989), 'Group treatment for women sex offenders against children', *Practice*, Summer, 118–159.
Becker, S. and MacPherson, S. (1986), *Poor clients. The extent and nature of financial poverty amongst consumers of social work services*, Nottingham University Benefits Research Unit.
Bentovim, Arnon, Elton, Anne, Hildebrand, Judy, Tranter, Marianne and Vizard, Eileen (1988), *Child sexual abuse within the family*, London: Wright.
Bettleheim (1979), *Surviving and other essays*, London: Thames & Hudson.
Brant, R. S. and Tisza, V. B. (1977), 'The sexually misused child', *American Journal of Orthopsychiatry*, 47, (80), January.

Brearley, Paul (1982), *Risk and social work hazards and helping*, Routledge and Kegan Paul.
Browne, A. (1987), *When battered women kill*, New York: Free Press.
Caffey, J (1946), 'Multiple fractures in the long bones of infants suffering from chronic subdural haemotoma', *A.J.R.*, **58**, 163–173.
Cantoni, Lucile (1981), 'Clinical issues in domestic violence', *Social Casework, The Journal of Contemporary Social Work*, 62, January.
Carlson, Bonnie (1991), 'Adolescents, forgotten victims of physical abuse', *Violence update*, London/Beverley Hills: Sage.
Chesterman, Mark (1985), 'Child sexual abuse and social work', *Social Work Today*, Norwich: UEA.
Christiansen, John and Blake, Reed (1990), 'The grooming process in father/daughter incest', in Anne Horton et al (eds), *The Incest Perpetrator, A family member no-one wants to treat*, London/Beverley Hills: Sage.
Corby, Brian (1987), *Working with child abuse*, Milton Keynes/Philadelphia: Open University Press.
Corder, Billie, Haizlip, Thomas, DeBoer, Pat (1990), 'A pilot study for a structured, time limited therapy group for sexually abused pre-adolescent children', *Child Abuse and Neglect*, **14**, 243–251.
Cowburn, Malcolm (1990), 'Assumptions about sex offenders', *Probation Journal*, March.
Cox, Tony (1978), *Stress*, London/Basingstoke: Macmillan.
Craig, Allen (1990), 'Women as perpetrators of child sexual abuse, recognition barriers', in Anne Horton et al (eds), *The incest perpetrator*, London/Beverley Hills: Sage.
Creighton, S. and Noyes, P. (1989), *Child abuse trends in England and Wales 1983–87*, London: NSPCC.
Crompton, Margaret (1980), 'Respecting children', in *Social work with young people*, London: Edward Arnold.
Dale, Peter (1986), *Dangerous families*, London: Tavistock Publications.
Davies, Murry, Waters, Jim, Dale, Peter, Morrison, Tony, Roberts, Wilf (1985), *Promoting change with child abusing families*, Rochdale Child Abuse Training Committee.
Day, Beryl (1983), *Meeting the needs of physically and emotionally neglected children*, London: NSPCC.

De Francis, V (1969), *Protecting the child victim of sex crimes committed by adults*, Denver: American Humane Association.

De Lang, C. (1986), 'The family place, children's therapeutic programme', *Children Today*, March/April, 12–15.

De Mause, L. (1974), 'The evolution of childhood', in L. De Mause (ed.) *The history of childhood*, New York: Harper and Row.

De Young, M. (1982), *The sexual victimization of children*, Jefferson, South Carolina: McFarland.

DoH (Department of Health) (1988), *Protecting children*, London: HMSO.

DoH (Department of Health) (1989a), *Introduction to The Children Act*, London: HMSO.

DoH (Department of Health) (1989b), *The care of children: principles and practice in regulations and guidance*, London: HMSO.

DoH (Department of Health) (1989c), *Working together under the 1989 Children Act*, London: HMSO.

DoH (Department of Health) (1991a), *The Children Act 1989 guidance and regulations vol. 1, Court Orders*, London: HMSO.

DoH (Department of Health) (1991b), *The Children Act 1989 guidance and regulations vol. 2, Family support, day care and educational provisions for young children*, London: HMSO.

DoH (Department of Health) (1991c), *Working together under the 1989 Children Act*, London: HMSO.

DHSS (Department of Health and Social Security) (1982), *Child abuse – a study of inquiry reports, 1973–81*, London: HMSO.

DHSS (Department of Health and Social Security (1985), *Social work decisions in child care – recent research findings and their implications*, London: HMSO.

Dingwall, R., Eekelaar, J. and Murray, T (1983), *The protection of children, state intervention and family life*, Oxford: Basil Blackwell.

Divine, David (1982/3), 'Like it or lump it', 5.11.82. 'Spinning the African web', 20.5.83. 'Beyond pathology', 8.7.83. 'Facts of black life', 7.83. 'Strengths of black life', 3.7.83. 'Melting pot or salad bowl', 29.7.83. All *Caribbean Times*.

Divine, David (1985), Submission to the Jasmine Beckford Enquiry.

Douglas, A. (1989), 'All you need to know to enjoy case conferences', *Social Work Today*, 16 March.

Doyle, Celia (1990), *Working with abused children*, London/Basingstoke: Macmillan.
Eekelaar, J. and Dingwall, R. (1990), *The reform of child care law*, London: Routledge.
Elbow, Margaret (1982), 'Children of violent marriages. The forgotten victims', *Social Casework*, 465–471.
Elton, Anne (1988), 'Family treatment – treatment methods and techniques', in A. Bentovim et al (eds), *Child sexual abuse within the family*, London: Wright.
Erooga, Marcus and Masson, Helen (1989), 'The silent volcano. Groupwork with mothers of sexually abused children', *Practice*, 3, (1), 24–38.
Erooga, Marcus and Masson, Helen (1990), *Investigations – journeys into the unknown*, Rochdale Child Protection Training Sub Committee.
Faller, Kathleen (1988a), 'Women who sexually abuse children', *Violence and Victims*, 2, (4).
Faller, Kathleen (1988b), *Child sexual abuse. An interdisciplinary manual for diagnosis case management and treatment*, London/Basingstoke: Macmillan.
Famulara, R., Stone, K., Barnum, R. and Wharton, R. (1986), 'Alcoholism and severe maltreatment', *American Journal of Orthopsychiatry*, 56, 481–485.
Faulk, M. (1974), 'Men who assault their wives', *Medicine Science and Law*, 14,180–183.
Fawcett, Judy (1987), 'The long road back to normality', *Community Care*, 29 October.
Finkelhor, David (1984), *Child sexual abuse. New theory and research*, New York: Free Press.
Finkelhor and Associates (1986), *A sourcebook on child sexual abuse*, London/Beverley Hills: Sage.
Finkelhor, D., Gelles, R. J., Hotaling, G. T. and Strauss, M. A. (eds) (1983), *The dark side of families. Current family violence research*, London/Beverley Hills: Sage.
Finkelhor, David, Williams, Linda and Burns, Nanci (1988), *Nursery Crimes*, London/Beverley Hills: Sage.
Forsstrom-Cohen, B. and Rosenbaum, A. (1985), 'The effects of parental marital violence on young adults, an exploratory investigation', *Journal of Marriage and Family*, 47, 467–471.
Freeman-Longo, R. E. (1987), *Child sexual abuse*, Des Moines, IA: Drake University.

Fromuth, M. E. (1986), 'The relationship of childhood sexual abuse with later psychological and sexual adjustment in a sample of college women', *Child Abuse and Neglect*, **10**, 5–15.

Furniss, Tillman (1991), *The multi-professional handbook of child sexual abuse*, London: Routledge.

Garbarino, James (1980), Gillian Gwen, *Understanding abusive families*, Toronto: Lexington Books.

Garbarino, James and Sherman, Deborah (1978), 'High risk neighbourhoods and high risk families', Nebraska Centre for the study of Youth Development, Mimeographed, quoted in *Damaged parents*, Polansky et al.

Garbarino, James and Sherman, Deborah (1980), 'High risk neighbourhoods and high risk families – the human ecology of child maltreatment (Boys Town Nebraska). Center for the study of youth development', *Child development*, **51**, 188–198.

Gary (1974), *A resource guide on black families in the USA*.

Gayford, J. J. (1975), 'Wife battering : A preliminary survey of 100 cases', *British Medical Journal*, 194–197.

Glaser, Danya and Frosh, Stephen (1988), *Child sexual abuse*, London/Basingstoke: Macmillan.

Gil, D. (1970), *Violence against children. Physical abuse in the United States*, Cambridge, Mass.: Harvard University.

Gil, D. (1975), Unravelling child abuse, *American Journal of Orthopsychiatry*, **45**, (3), 346–56.

Green, A. (1978), 'Self destructive behaviour in battered children', *American Journal of Psychiatry*, **135**, (5), May, 579–82.

Greenland, Cyril (1987), *Preventing CAN deaths*, London/New York: Tavistock Publications.

Groth, N. and Russell, D. (1984), Quoted in *Child sexual abuse*, Finkelhor David (ed.) New York: Free Press.

Hall, Liz and Lloyd, Siobhan (1989), *Surviving child sexual abuse*, Lewis: The Falmer Press.

Harrison, P. A., Lumry, A. E. and Claypatch, C. (1984), 'Female sexual abuse victims. Perspective on family dysfunction substance use and psychiatric disorders'. Paper presented at 2nd national conference for family violence researchers, Durham, New Hampshire.

Hatchett, Will (1991), 'Under pressure', *Community Care*, 18 April.

Herrenkohl, R. C., Herrenkohl, E. C. and Egolf, B. P. (1983), 'Circumstances surrounding the occurrence of child maltreatemnt', *Journal of Consulting and Clinical Psychology*, **51**, 424–431.

Herzberg, F. (1968), *Work and the nature of man*, London: Staples Press.

Hilberman, E. and Munson, K. (1977), 'Sixty battered women', *Victimology International Journal*, **2**, 460–470.

Hinchey, Frances and Gavelek, James (1982), 'Empathetic responding in children of battered mothers', *Child Abuse and Neglect*, **6**, 395–401.

Hoffman, L. R. (1965), 'Group problem solving', in L. Berkowitz (ed.) *Advances in experimental psychology vol. 2*, London: Academic Press.

Horton, Anne, Johnson, Barry, Roundy, Lynn and Williams, Doran (eds) (1990), *The incest perpetrator. A family member no-one wants to treat*, London/Beverley Hills: Sage.

House of Commons (1984), *Second report from the Social Services Committee, Session 1983–1984, Children in Care HC 360*, London: HMSO.

Howing, Phyllis et al (1987), 'Effective intervention to ameliorate the incidence of child maltreatment. The empirical base', reproduced in *Social Work*, July 1989.

Hughes, H. M. (1982), 'Brief interventions with children in a battered wives shelter, a model preventive programme', *Family Relations*, **31**, 495–502.

Hughes, H. M. (1986), 'Research with children in shelters, implications for clinical services', *Children Today*, 21–25.

Husband, C. (1991), 'Race conflictual politics and antiracist social work: lessons from the past for action in the 90's', in *Setting the context for change*, pp. 46–73. London: Antiracist Social Work for Education/CCETSW.

Irvine, Rob (1988), 'Child abuse and poverty', in Becker, Saul and Macpherson, Stewart (eds), *Public Issues and Private Pain, Social Services Insight*, London.

Jaffe, P., Wilson, S. and Wolfe, D. (1989), 'Specific assessment and intervention strategies for children exposed to wife batterers', *Canadian Journal of Mental Health*, **7**, 157–163.

Jaffe, Peter, Wolfe, David, Wilson, Susan Kaye (1990), *Children of battered women*, London/Beverley Hills: Sage.

James, J. and Meyerding, J. (1977), 'Early sexual experiences and prostitution', *American Journal of Psychiatry*, **134**, 1381–1385.

Jones, David, Pickett, John, Oates, Margaret and Barber, Peter (1987), *Understanding child abuse*, London: Macmillan.

Jones, J., Butler, H., Hamilton, K., Perdue, J., Stern, H. and Woody, R. (1986), 'Munchausen syndrome by proxy', *Child Abuse and Neglect*, **10**, 33–40.

Jordan, B. (1976), *Freedom and the welfare state*, London: Routledge and Kegan Paul.

Justice, Blair and Justice, Rita (1979), *The Broken Taboo – sex in the family*, London: Peter Owen.

Kane, R. A. (1975), *Interpersonal teamwork*, Manpowers Monograph no 81: Syracuse University School of Social Work.

Kaplan, Stephen and Wheeler, Eugenie (1983), 'Survival skills for working with potentially violent clients', *Social Casework*, 339–346.

Kempe, C. H. et al (1962), 'The battered child syndrome', *J.A.M.A.* **181**, (1), 17–24.

Kempe, C. and Helfer, R. (1972), *Helping the battered child and his family*, Philadelphia: Lippincott.

Kempe, Ruth and Kempe, Henry (1978), *Child abuse – the developing child*, London: The Open University Press/Fontana Open Books.

Korbin, Jill (1981), *Child abuse and neglect – cross cultural perspectives*, University of California Press.

Kotelchuk, M. (1982), 'Child abuse and neglect – prediction and misclarification', in R. Starr (ed.) *Child abuse predictions, Policy implications*, pp. 67–104. Cambridge: Ballinger.

Krugman, Richard, Lenherr, Marilyn, Betz, Lynn and Fryer, George (1986), 'The relationship between unemployment and physical abuse of children', *Child Abuse and Neglect*, **10**, 415–418.

Kadushin, Alfred (1976), *Supervision in social work*, New York: Columbia University Press.

Lally, J. Ronald (1984), '3 views of child neglect: expanding visions of preventative intervention', *Child Abuse and Neglect*, **8**, 243–254.

Lask, B. (1987), 'From honeymoon to reality', *Journal of Family Therapy*, **9**, 303.

Law Commission (1987), *Care supervision and interim orders in custody proceedings. Working together, paper No. 100*, London: HMSO.

Leach, Penelope (1990), 'Children in society – listening to children', in Anne Bannister, Kevin Barrett and Eileen Shearer (eds), Harlow: Longman.

Leighton, B. (1989), *Spousal abuse in metropolitan Toronto, Report No. 1989.02*, Ottowa: Solicitor General of Canada.

Levine, M. B. (1975), 'Inter-parental violence and its effect on the children. A study of 50 families in general practice', *Medicine Science and the Law*, **15**, (3), 172–176.

Lorber, R. Fellon, D. K. and Reid, J. M. (1984), 'A social learning approach to the reduction of coercial processes in child abusive families. A molecular analysis', *Advances in Behaviour Research and Therapy*, **6**, 29–45.

Lorde, A. (1981), 'An open letter to Mary Daly', in E. D. C. Moraga and G. Anzaldua (eds), *This bridge called my back-writings by radical women of colour*, pp. 94–97, Persephone.

Lynch, M. A. and Roberts, J. (1982), *Consequences of child abuse*, London/New York: Academic Press.

Lynch, Margaret (1988), 'The consequences of child abuse,' in Kevin Browne, Cliff Davies and Peter Strattan (eds), *Early prediction and prevention of child abuse*, Wiley and Sons.

Macfarlane, Kee, Waterman, Jill, Conerly, Shawn, Damon, Linda, Durfee, Michael and Long, Suzanne (1986), *Sexual abuse of young children*, London/Sydney: Holt Rinehart and Winston.

Macleod, L. (1987), *Battered not beaten ... preventing wife battering in Canada*, Ottawa: Canadian Advisory Council on the Status of Women.

Marchant, R. (1991), 'Myths and facts about sexual abuse and children with disabilities', *Child Abuse Review*, **5**, (2), Summer.

Martin, H. and Beezley, P. (1977), 'Behavioural observations of abused children', *Developmental Medicine and Child Neurology*, **19**, 373–83.

Martin, H., Beezley, P., Conway, E. and Kemp, C. H. (1974), 'The development of abused children', *Advances in Paediatrics*, **21**, 25–73.

Mathews, Ruth, Matthews, Jane and Spettz, Kathleen (1989), *Female sexual offenders*, The Safer Society Press.

Mathis, James (1972), *Clear thinking about sexual deviations*, London: Nelson Holt.

McCormack, A., Janus, M. D. and Burgess, A. V. (1986), 'Runaway youths and sexual victimization. Gender differences in an adolescent runaway population.' *Child Abuse and Neglect*, 10, 378–395.

McGuire, James and Priestley, Philip (1991), *Offending behaviour – skills and stratagems for going straight*, London: Batsford.

Meadow, R. (1977), 'Munchausen Syndrome by Proxy. The hinterland of child abuse', *Lancet* 57, 92–98.

Meadow, R. (1982), 'Munchausen Syndrome by Proxy', *Archives of disease in childhood* 57, 92, 98.

Meadow, R. (1985), 'Management of Munchausen syndrome by proxy', *Archives of Disease in Childhood*, 60, 385–393.

Mehl, Albert, Coble, Larry and Johnson, Scott (1990), 'Munchausen syndrome by proxy – a family affair', *Child Abuse and Neglect*, 14, 577–585.

Meinig, Mary and Bonner, Barbara (1990), 'Returning the treated sex offender to the family', *Violence Update*, London: Sage.

Millham, S., Bullock, R., Hosie, K. and Haak, M. (1986), *Lost in care – the problems of maintaining links between children in care and their families*, Aldershot: Gower.

Milner, J. S. and Wimberley, R. C. (1980), 'Prediction and explanation of child abuse', *Journal of Clinical Psychology*, 36, 875–884.

Monahan, J. and Cummings, L. (1975), 'Social policy implications of the inability to predict violence', *Journal of Social Issues*, 31, (2), 153–64.

Mones, Paul (1985), 'The relationship between child abuse and patricide', in Eli Newberger (ed.), *Unhappy families*, Massachusetts: P.S.G. Publishing Company.

Moore, J. (1975a), 'Yo yo children', *International Child Welfare Review*, no. 25, May, 19–24.

Moore, J. (1975b), 'Yo yo children, victims of marital violence', *Child Welfare*, L1V, (8), Sept/Oct, 557–566.

Moore, J. (1982), 'Like a rabbit caught in headlights', *Community Care*, 4 November.

Moore, J. (1984), 'None so blind', *Community Care*, 26 April.

Moore, J. (1986), 'All in the family', *Community Care*, 1 May.

Moore, J. (1990), 'Confronting the perpetrator', *Community Care*, 12 April.

Moore, J., Galcius, A. and Pettican, K. (1981), 'Emotional risk to children caught in violent matrimonial conflict. The Basildon treatment project', *Child Abuse and Neglect*, **5**, 147–152.

Morrison, Tony (1990), 'The emotional effects of child protection work on the worker', *Practice*, **4**, (4).

Murphy, Solbritt, Orkow, Bonnie and Nicola, Ray (1985), 'Prenatal prediction of child abuse and neglect. A prospective study', *Child Abuse and Neglect*, **9**, 225–235.

Murray, Margaret (1963), *The splendour that was Egypt*, London: Book Club Associates/Sidgwick & Jackson Ltd.

Oates, Kim (1990) *Understanding and managing child sexual abuse*, Sydney: W. B. Saunders/Bailliere Tindall/Harcourt Brace Jovanovich.

Oates, R. K., Forrest, D. and Peacock, A. (1985), 'Self esteem of abused children', *Child Abuse and Neglect*, **9**, 159–163.

O'Connell, Michael, Leberg, Eric and Donaldson, Craig (1990), *Working with sex offenders. Guidelines for therapy selection*, London/Beverley Hills: Sage.

Okine, E. (1990), 'Planning for black children in care', seminar notes.

Okine, E. (1991), 'The needs of black children in care: issues of fostering and adoption', MA research.

Orkow, Bonnie (1985), 'Implementation of a family stress checklist', *Child Abuse and Neglect*, **9**, 405–410.

O'Toole, R. and Nalephac, P. (1983), 'Professional knowledge and diagnosis of child abuse', in D. Finkelhor, et al (eds), *The dark side of families, Current family violence*, London/Beverley Hills: Sage.

Palmer, A. J. and Yoshimura, G. J. (1984), 'Munchausen Syndrome by Proxy', *Journal of American Academy of Child Psychiatry*, **23**, 503–508.

Pfouts, J. H., Schopler, J. H. and Henley, H. C. Jnr (1982), 'Forgotten victims of family violence', *Social Work*, **27**, 367–368.

Pines, Alaya, Aronson, Elliott and Kafry, Ditsa (1981), *Burnout from tedium to personal growth*, New York: Free Press.

Polansky, Norman (1986), *Treating loneliness in child protection*, Child Welfare League of America.

Polansky, Norman, Ammons, Paul and Gaudin, James Jnr., (1985) 'Loneliness and isolation in child neglect', *Social Casework*, **66**, (1).

Polansky, Norman, Chalmers, Mary, Williams, David and Buttenwieser, Elizabeth (1981), *Damaged parents – an anatomy of child neglect*, The University of Chicago Press.

Polansky, N. A., Hally, C. and Polansky, N. F. (1975), *Profile of neglect*, Washington DC Public Services, Dept of HEW.

Pruitt, D. G. (1971), 'Choice shifts in group discussion – an introductory review', *Journal of Personality and Social Psychology*, **20**, (3), 339–360.

Redgrave, Ken (1987), *Childs Play. Direct work with the deprived child*, Cheadle: Boys and Girls Welfare Society.

Robin, Michael (1982), 'The sheltering arms. The roots of child protection', in Eli Newberger (ed.), *Child abuse*, Boston: Little Brown & Company.

Rosenberg, M. S. (1984), 'Intergenerational family violence. A critique and implications for witnessing children', paper presented at the 92nd annual convention of the American Association Toronto.

Rowe, J. (1989), 'Caring concern', *The Guardian* 2.6.89.

Rowett, C. (1986), *Violence in the context of local authority social work*, Cambridge: Institute of Criminology.

Ryan, Gail (1987), 'Juvenile sex offenders – development and correction', *Child Abuse and Neglect*, **11**, 385–395.

Salter, Anna (1988) *Treating child sex offenders and victims – A practical guide*, London/Beverley Hills: Sage.

Scavo, Rebecca (1989), 'Female adolescent sex offenders, A neglected treatment group', *Social Casework*.

Schechter, M. D. and Roberge, L. (1976), 'Sexual exploitation', in R. C. Helfer and C. H. Kempe (eds), *Child Abuse and neglect, the family and the community*, Cambridge, Mass: Ballinger.

Schmitt, B. D. (1978), *The child protection team handbook*, pp83–108, New York and London: Garland.

Sebold, John (1987), 'Indicators of child sexual abuse in males', *Social Casework, Journal of contemporary social work*, February, 75–80.

Seligman, M. E. P. (1975), *Helplessness on depression, development and death*, San Francisco: W. H. Freeman.

Sgroi, Suzanne (1975), 'Child sexual molestation', *Children Today*, **44**, 18–21.

Sgroi, Suzanne (1982), *Handbook of clinical intervention in child sexual abuse*, Massachusetts/Toronto: Lexington Books.
Shearer, Eileen (1990), 'Child abuse investigation', in Anne Bannister, Kevin Barrett and Eileen Shearer (eds), *Listening to children, the professional response to hearing the abused child*, Harlow: Longman.
Silverman, F. N. (1953) 'The Roentgen manifestations of unrecognised skeletal trauma in infants', *AJR*, **69**, 413.
Sluckin, W. (1983), *Maternal bonding*, Oxford: Basil Blackwell.
Smith, Lorna (1989), *Domestic violence research study 107*, London: DHSS.
Smith, S. M. and Hanson, R. (1980), 'Interpersonal relationships and child rearing practices in 214 parents of battered children', in J. Cook and R. T. Bowles (eds), *Child abuse commission and ommission*, pp. 235-254, London: Butterworth.
Sopp-Gilson, S. (1980), 'Children from violent homes', *Journal of Ontario Association of Childrens Aid Societies*, **23**, (10), 1-5.
Steele, B. (1987), 'Psychodynamic factors in child abuse', in R. E. Helfer and R. S. Kempe (eds), *The battered child*, 4th edn, pp. 81-114, University of Chicago Press.
Stevenson, Olive (1986), 'Book review of the politics of child abuse', *Journal of Social Policy*, **15**, (1), 119-121.
Stevenson, Olive (1988) 'Multidisciplinary work – where next?', *Child Abuse Review*, **2**, (1).
Stevenson, Olive (1989) *Child abuse – public policy and professional practice*, New York: Harvester Wheatsheaf.
Stoner, J. A. F. (1961), 'A comparison of individuals and group decisions involving risk' quoted in Pruitt (1971).
Straus, M. A., Gelles, R. J. and Steinmetz, S. K. (1980), *Behind closed doors. Violence in the American family*. Garden City: Doubleday Press.
Strenz, T. (1980), 'The Stockholm Syndrome – law enforcement policy and ego defences of the hostage', *Annals of the New York Sciences*, no 347, 137-150.
Stroud, John (1974), 'Remember Maria NO, remember Emma', *Community Care*, 11 September.
Summit, R. C. (1983), 'The child sexual abuse accommodation syndrome', *Child Abuse and Neglect*, **7**, 177-193.

Summit, Roland and Kryso (1978), 'Sexual abuse of children. A clinical spectrum', *American Journal of Orthopsychiatry*, **48**, (2), April.
Tannen, Deborah (1990), *You just don't understand – women and men in conversation*, London: Virago.
Tolstoy, Leo (1828–1910), *Anna Karenin*, many editions.
Tong, L., Oates, R. K. and McDowell, M. (1987), 'Personality development following sexual abuse', *Child Abuse and Neglect*, **11**, 371–383.
Tonge, W. L., James, D. S. and Susan, Hillam (1975), *Families without hope. A controlled study of 33 problem families*, Royal College of Psychiatrists: Headley Bro Ltd.
TUFTS (1984), *New England Medical Centre Division of Child Psychiatry. Sexually exploited children service and research project*, US Department of Justice: Washington D.C.
UNICEF (1989), *UN Convention on The Rights of The Child*.
Vore, D. (1973), 'Prenatal nutrition and post-natal intellectual development', *Merrill Palmer Quarterly*, **19**, 253–260.
Walker, C., Bonner, B. and Kaufman, K. (1988), *The physically and sexually abused child. Evaluation and treatment*, Oxford: Pergamon Press.
Wardlaw, G. (1982), *Political terrorism. Theory tactics and counter measures*, Cambridge University Press.
Wardle, M. (1975), '(Crompton) hippopotamus or cow. On not communicating about children.' *Social Work Today*, **6** (14).
Westra, B. L. and Martin, H. P. (1981), 'Children of battered women', *Matern. Child. Nurs. J.*, **10**, 41–51.
Whipple, Ellen and Webster-Stratton, Carolyn (1991), 'The role of parental stress in physically abusive families', *Child Abuse and Negelct*, **15**, 279–291.
Wilson, S., Cameron, S., Jaffe, P. and Wolfe, D. (1989), 'Children exposed to wife abuse', *Social Casework*, **70**, 180–184.
Wolfe, D. A., Zak, L., Wilson, S. and Jaffe, P. (1986), 'Child witnesses of violence between parents. Critical issues in behavioural and social adjustment', *Journal of Abnormal Child Psychology*, 14.1.95. 104.
Wolock, Isabel and Horowitz (1984), 'Child maltreatment as a social problem', *American Journal of Orthopsychiatry*, **54**, (4), October.
Wyre, Ray (1989), 'Working with the paedophile', *ISTD*

Understanding the paedophile. Conference Papers.
Young, Leontine (1981), *Physical child neglect*, Chicago National Committee for Prevention of Child Abuse.

REPORTS

Beckford, Jasmine (1985)
A Child in Trust – The report of the Panel of Inquiry into the circumstances surrounding the death of *Jasmine Beckford*, London Borough of Brent.

Carlile, Kimberley (1987)
A Child in Mind – The report of the Commission of Inquiry into the circumstances surrounding the death of *Kimberley Carlile*, London Borough of Greenwich.

Chapman, Lester (1979)
Inquiry Report. Report of an independent inquiry commissioned by the County Council and Area Health Authorities of Berkshire and Hampshire.

Clark, Richard (1975)
Report of the Committee of Inquiry into the consideration given and steps taken towards securing the welfare of *Richard Clark* by Perth Town Council and other bodies or persons concerned, HMSO.

Cleveland Report (1988)
Report of the Inquiry into child abuse in *Cleveland* 1987. HMSO.

Colwell, Maria (1974)
Department of Health – Report of the Committee of Inquiry into the care and supervision provided in relation to *Maria Colwell*, HMSO.

Gates, Lucy (1982)
The Lucy Gates Family Inquiry. Findings, explanations and recommendations, London Boroughs of Bexley and Greenwich and Bexley Heath Authority.

Henry, Tyra (1987)
Whose Child – A report of the Public Inquiry into the death of *Tyra Henry*, London Borough of Lambeth.

Mason, Doreen (1989)
The Doreen Aston Report – Commissioned by A.R.C. Lambeth Lewisham and Southwark, July, London Borough of Lewisham.

Meurs, Steven (1975)
   Report of the Review Body appointed to inquire into the death of *Steven Meurs*, Norfolk Social Services Department.

Page, Malcolm (1981)
   Report by the Panel appointed by the Essex A.R.C., Essex County Council.

Spencer, Karen (1978)
   Report by Professor J. D. McClean, Professor of Law at the University of Sheffield, Derbyshire Social Services Department.

Sukina (1991)
   An evaluation report of the circumstances leading to her death. The Bridge Child Care Consultancy Service, London.

Index

abuse, *see* child abuse;
　　emotional abuse; physical
　　abuse; sexual abuse
abusers, 18–21, 59, 60
　　see also parents,
　　　　characteristics of
　　　　abusing;
　　　　perpetrators
ACPC (Area Child Protection
　　Committee) 25, 164, 168
adolescents
　　as victims 15–16
　　as abusers, *see*
　　　　perpetrators,
　　　　young
ageism 176
anger 35, 98, 106, 130, 137
　　see also guilt
anonymous referrals, *see*
　　referrals
anti-discriminatory practice
　　115, 118, 121
anxiety, effects of 32
assessment 33–5, 114, 115, 116,
　　120–21, 180–83, *see also*
　　misassessment
authority 25–6
　　as a therapeutic tool 26,
　　　　155–6
　　professional 26, 158–9
　　statutory 25–7, 144–6,
　　　　158–9

Beckford, Jasmine 3, 36, 110
　　see also inquiry reports
black families, *see* working with
　　black families
bonding 18
Brewer, Wayne 33
burnout 104–5, 160, 161

Caffey, John 15
care orders 146, 152
care proceedings 150–52
Carlile, Kimberley 3, 128
　　see also inquiry reports
case conference, *see* child
　　protection conferences
chair of conference, *see* child
　　protection conferences
Chapman, Lester 102, 128
　　see also inquiry reports
child abuse 92–3, 162–78
　　causes of physical abuse
　　　　14–24

199

effects of 4–10, 101–2,
  180–83
 historical perspective 15
 marital violence as 37–45
 physical effects of 9
 types of *see* emotional
  abuse; neglect;
  physical abuse;
  sexual abuse
child assessment order 146, 150
child protection conferences
  92–3, 120, 121, 162–8
 chairing 164, 167, 170,
  177–8
 children at 163–4
 decision-making at
  167–9
 membership of 170–72
 minutes of 178
 parents at 163–4
 problems of 164–70,
  171–3
child protection plan 35, 36,
  163, 173, 183
Child Protection Register 23,
  163
child protection skills 154–61
 see also therapeutic
  methods/tools
children
 abused 3–10, 47–8, 81–2,
  127–39
 black children in care
  122–3
 hyperactive 5, 17, 84
 ice-centred 7
 neglected 81–4
 passive 6
 rights of 25–6
 sexually abused 47–8
 welfare of 127
 working with 44–5, 62–4,
  91–2, 127–39, 161
Children Act 1989 115, 117,
 118, 127, 140, 142–53, 162

Clarke, Darryn 33
 see also inquiry reports
classification 102
classism 3, 175–6
Cleveland Report *see* inquiry
 reports
Colwell, Maria 25, 33, 127–8
 see also inquiry reports
communication
 interdisciplinary 59
 with children 128–9,
  131–9
 with parents 155
confidentiality 28, 134
conflict 35–6, 38
 by proxy 105, 168
corporal punishment 16
courts 142–4, 146–8
cultural factors 24

dangerousness, predicting 34
data 31
DAZPOE 30–36
denial 66–7, 165
depression 99, 100
disabilityism 176
doctors 170
dominant ideas 102–3, 130
drift, danger of 36, 100, 154,
 173

emergency protection order
 145, 146, 148–9
emotional abuse 52
 marital violence as a
  form of 37–45
  passim
Eurocentric view 116, 117
evaluation 36

false beliefs 174–7
family
 history 31
 isolation 40
 patterns or systems 22–3,
  70–71, 180–83

physically abusing 25
working with sexually
abusing family
60–73, 79
family work 69–71
see also working with
black families
fostering, as a dominant idea
103
recruiting black foster
parents 122–3
frozen watchfulness 7, 102

games
clients play 27–8, 90–91,
158–9
workers play 108–10,
166–7, 171–3
GAL *see* guardian *ad litem*
Gates, Lucy *see* inquiry reports
gender issues 43, 107, 119, 175
see also sexism
grooming 54
groupwork 62, 69, 89
guardian *ad litem* (GAL) 148
guidelines 164, 178
guilt
in abused child 7–9, 41
anger 98

helpers *see* workers
helping the abused child *see*
children, working with
Henry, Tyra 3, 103
see also inquiry reports
hostility, working with 159–60
hyperactive children *see*
children, hyperactive

ice-centred children, *see*
children, ice-centred
ILSW (Integration of Law and
Social Work) approach 27,
157, 159
impotence 98, 99, 102
see also omnipotence/
impotence

incest
endogamous 53
misogynous 56
inquiry reports
Beckford, Jasmine 3,
25–6, 141, 155, 166
Carlile, Kimberley 3, 97,
99, 128, 141
Chapman, Lester 102,
128
Colwell, Maria 25, 32,
33, 127–8
Clarke, Richard 154
Cleveland 127, 141
Gates, Lucy 94
Henry, Tyra 3, 103, 175,
176
Mason, Doreen 94
Meurs, Stephen 94
Page, Malcolm 94, 154
Piazzani, Max 33
Spencer, Karen 154
Sukina 8
Taylor, Carly 33
institutional racism *see* racism
interdisciplinary work 59, 105,
117, 160, 165–6, 169–70
interpreters, use of 117, 120
investigation 27, 30–36, 116–17
duty to investigate 146–7

Kempe, Henry 15, 47, 109
keyworker 36, 163, 169

law 140–53, 168
see also ILSW
learned helplessness 99–100
local authorities
duties of 144–6
powers of 25
Lockhart, Emma 25
losing cards 34–5

marital conflict 20
marital violence 37–45
children as victims of
40–42

effects on child 38–43
extent of 45
marital work/counselling 44–5, 69–71
marriage, patterns of 37–8
Mason, Doreen *see* inquiry reports
media *see* press
mental illness 21
Meurs, Stephen *see* inquiry reports
misassessment, of black families 114, 115, 118
    avoiding 120–21
mothers of abused children, working with 61–2, 68, 86–9
Munchausen syndrome by proxy 20

NSPCC (National Society for the Prevention of Cruelty to Children) 40, 159, 169, 177
neglect 80–94
    definition of 82
    causes of 82–3
    working with neglected children 91–2
    working with neglecting parents 86–91

omnipotence/impotence 98
operational plan *see* child protection plan

paedophile 56
Page, Malcolm *see* inquiry reports
parental extensions 7
parental responsibility 142, 145, 151
Parents
    characteristics of abusing parents 18–21, 22, 26, 35, 158, 180–83
    games parents play 27–28
    in child protection conferences *see* child protection conferences
    mentally ill 21
    neglectful 84–5
    non-abusing 47, 53–4, 61
    planning with 36
        see also planning
    teaching parenting skills to 35, 89
    working with 86–9, 155
        see also family; neglect; sexual abuse
passive children *see* children
perpetrators (of sexual abuse) 46–7, 51–7, 59, 60
    women as 46, 73–6
    working with male perpetrators 64–9
    working with female perpetrators 76–8
    young perpetrators 49, 79
physical abuse 13–36
Piazzani, Max *see* inquiry reports
'pickup' of family feelings 97–9
place of safety order *see* emergency protection order
planning 35–6, 60–61
    see also child protection plan
play 89
police
    and discrimination 119
    joint work with 33, 119
    PACE (Police and Criminal Evidence Act) 150

powers of 149–50, 169
police protection order 149
poverty *see* stress factors
precipitating events *see* trigger factors
predictors *see* losing cards
press, role of 25
probation officers 59, 171
procedures *see* guidelines
professionals
    cooperation 59
    self-work 59
protection plan *see* child protection plan

racism 3, 24, 110–13, 114–24 *passim*, 174–5
    institutional 112, 115, 123
    see also black families, working with
recovery order 150
referrals, anonymous 28, 32
registers *see* Child Protection Register
removal from home 45, 103
risk
    assessment 34, 66–8, 72, 92–3
    in decision-making 66, 167, 169–70
    types of 34, 169
ritual abuse 57–9
role reversal 19
'rule of optimism' 170

scapegoating 41
school, problems at 41
    reports 117, 121
secrecy 40, 47, 54, 79
self-work 59–60, 127–9
sexism 3, 38, 175
sexual abuse 46–79
    causes of 50–55 *passim*
    definition of 48–50

    effects of 55–6, 62–4
    indicators of 50–51
    male victims of 55
    mothers and 47, 53–4
    types of 49–50, 52–3, 57–8, 73
    working with families in 59–73, 79
sexual abusers *see* perpetrators
siblings, of abused children 3, 61, 68, 79, 171, 181
Silverman, Fred 15
skills *see* child protection skills; social workers, skills of
social workers
    and authority 25, 155
    skills of 154–61
social work methods *see* children, working with; parents, working with; self-work; sexual abuse, working with families; therapeutic methods
stereotyping 103, 165
stress factors 35
    poverty 23
    social isolation 24
    unemployment 14
    see also trigger factors
suicide attempts 9
Sukina *see* inquiry reports
supervision of workers 106–10, 120, 156
    training for 107
    types of 106–8
supervision order 146, 151, 152
support groups 120
survivors 9–10

Taylor, Carly *see* inquiry reports
teachers 117–18
teams 105, 160
therapeutic methods
    in marital work 44–5
    in sexual abuse 60–72

therapeutic tools 26, 87–8,
154–61 *passim*
see also child protection
skills
third objects 134
exercises using 135–9
trigger factors 14, 24, 180–83
see also stress factors

unemployment *see* stress factors

victim
parents as 27
victim/victimiser
syndrome 100–102
violence
children and 41–2
fear of 29
followed by affection 20,
22
in sexual abuse 57
marital *see* marital
violence
response to 29–30, 159–
60
stages of 29–30

wives, battered 37–45 *passim*
women
as perpetrators of sexual
abuse *see*
perpetrators
position of 24
role of, in sexual abuse
53–4
workers 25–7, 97–113
stress on 29, 161
working with black families
112, 114–124

yo-yo syndrome 40

'zoom in' 35